QUALITY, BEHAVIOR, AND THE BOTTOM LINE

The Human Side of Quality Improvement

Jerry Pounds

Tom Werner

Bob Foxworthy

Daniel Moran

jerry.pounds@qualitysafetyedge.com

DEDICATION

This book is for all the quality professionals, frontline employees, and managers who strive every day to improve quality in their organizations. We hope that this book provides some helpful ideas to enhance their efforts.

"*Quality, Behavior, and the Bottom Line*" has answered the hidden secrets to creating a true Quality culture. It is compelling, succinct and focuses on behavioral-based continuous improvement. As a student of the business, this is my reference book to establish, reinforce, and reward the correct behaviors."
—Kevin Walsh, Chief Operating Officer, Industrial Piping, Inc.

"This book outlines the considerations commonly overlooked by the quality processes that we spend millions of dollars on—the behaviors of the people adopting the processes. The authors provide a detailed understanding of where quality processes typically break down and how they work better with a focus on the right behaviors."
—Barry W. Ditzler, Director, Fukushima Modifications for Entergy Nuclear, CB&I

"This book will significantly enhance any improvement or quality initiative with clear and easy (but often overlooked) behavioral steps focusing on the critical-to-quality behaviors of the people who execute the work."
—Andrew Armpriester, manager, Fortune 10 energy company

"Finally, a book that ties together the lessons learned from systematically applying behavioral science in safety to another discipline—quality. People need to be part of the solution in an organization: it is a huge driver of continuous improvement. This book provides a blueprint for engaging employees in a behavior-based quality 'system,' a system that can provide significant quality improvement for any organization."
—Brian Duffy, Director of Corporate Environmental Manufacturing Safety, Crown Equipment Corporation

TABLE OF CONTENTS

ACKNOWLEDGMENTS

We greatly appreciate the friends and colleagues who read this book in draft form and provided extremely helpful advice and expert feedback.

We are grateful to Terry McSween, PhD the CEO of Quality Safety Edge for his guidance, input, and feedback throughout the writing of the book. We also thank Gail Snyder for her expert editing and advice.

Finally, we thank all of our colleagues at Quality Safety Edge for their support and their pioneering work in applying the behavioral approach to the workplace.

PREFACE

The international business landscape is littered with expensive quality improvement initiatives that have not met expectations and have been cast aside. Lean, Six Sigma, World Class Manufacturing, Operational Excellence, and Total Quality Management are still in fashion in spite of their mixed record. Some companies are implementing three or four initiatives at once—thinking more is better.

If you review each initiative, you see dozens of techniques, tools, and processes for solving problems and improving quality. Each initiative mentions frontline employees, but doesn't produce a systematic approach for addressing the role people play in hindering or improving quality.

The irony is that *frontline employees' behavior* is the fundamental element in producing a product or service. How frontline employees behave—doing things right, doing things wrong, not doing what they should—determines quality results. But quality initiatives have no systematic method for identifying or changing frontline employee behavior. This book provides a

1

systematic process for analyzing frontline employee behavior and identifying the specific behaviors each frontline employee should perform to accelerate quality improvement.

This book is a must-read for anyone who has implemented a quality improvement initiative but has not achieved or sustained the desired results. We know why the results are lacking or unsustainable. All quality doctrines call for supportive senior executives to ingrain quality practices into the organizational culture, but the initiatives do not specify how to do so.

Try this test. Open *any* book about Total Quality Management, continuous improvement, Lean, Six Sigma, World Class Manufacturing, or the Toyota Production System. Look for a chapter about "how to manage human behavior"—a chapter that describes exactly what supervisors and managers should say and do to influence the frontline employees' behaviors that are required to deliver high-quality results. You won't find one! Human behavior is not on the quality agenda. Quality gurus are often statisticians and engineers and designers who are not trained in how to encourage people to perform at their best.

When audiences asked Dr. W. Edwards Deming, the pioneering father of quality, what exactly managers should do to achieve his 14 Points, he would famously reply, "You're the manager; you figure it out." That mindset has continued in the world of quality. Quality initiatives primarily focus on analyzing data and designing processes and then count on managers to make quality plans come alive in the everyday work habits of frontline employees in the real-world workplace. Quality initiatives leave it up to managers to "figure it out."

Many quality initiatives have a gap—a missing ingredient, a blind spot. The gap is the assumption that human beings will automatically behave in accord with a newly designed quality procedure. Human behavior doesn't work that way! This book is about how to improve quality improvement by managing the essential human behavior element in quality plans. This book describes how to "figure it out."

Quality Improvement and Quality Initiatives

Changing the way we do things is often accompanied by uncertainty, frustration, and the desire to revert back to doing things the old way. At work and in our private lives, changing our behavior is not usually comfortable or easy. Doing things differently requires us to go through a *learning curve*—a term that embodies all the negative feelings we experience when struggling to improve.

Making changes in our private lives provides us with some insights into what to expect when we are asked to change our work behavior—the way we are used to doing things. When trying to lose weight or begin exercising, we find that measurement is essential to keeping ourselves committed and motivated. We count calories, count the number of minutes or miles we walk or run, record the amount of weight we lift to get stronger, or the amount of seconds we hold a stretch when trying to improve flexibility.

Measurement allows us to track change and provides us with encouraging feedback—information that motivates us and keeps us on track. Seeing our improvement gives us a good feeling; we are proud when we are successful. If others make supportive statements about our progress, this provides us with another dimension of pride and motivation toward our goal.

The same factors—measurement, feedback, and recognition—which we refer to as the *behavioral approach*, ensure that quality initiatives will be successfully implemented and the quality improvement plans they produce will be executed effectively. These factors need to be applied to the efforts of managers, supervisors, and frontline employees as they attempt to do new things, both individually and in team activities.

The main thing to be aware of is that training alone does not ensure that the new ways will stick. Training is the beginning; the behavioral approach adds the coaching of performers with measurement of their progress, positive feedback for the change, and recognition for their improvement.

1 APPLYING THE BEHAVIORAL APPROACH TO QUALITY

Many organizations use one or more of the popular quality-focused initiatives like Lean, Six Sigma, and World Class Manufacturing. Perhaps your company has invested time and effort in one of these approaches, or you use an eclectic combination of these tools and have seen them recycled through your organization over time.

You might find the following scenario familiar:

> An industrial component factory is experiencing a crisis in quality on the manufacturing lines. A large number of components are being kicked back for rework because of a quality issue, and customers are returning some of the machines that actually went out the door. The cost of rework, customer replacement, and customer retention has completely eroded the company's profit margin. The manufacturer is desperate.

They already have Lean and a version of Six Sigma in place, but the resource requirements for implementing these processes are slowly disintegrating for several reasons, one of which may be due to the distractions of quality issues. Although some of the quality issues are related to aging equipment and imprecise calibration, it becomes clear that human performance is the biggest cause. Machine operators are not doing their jobs as managers expect and supervisors are struggling to meet standard work expectations because of the number of unplanned workflow interruptions.

If the managers at this component factory witnessed operators doing the work, they would see that the operators have developed habitual shortcuts enabling them to do the job more quickly—saving them extra motion, energy, and allowing them to take longer breaks. This type of behavior is not unusual for frontline employees, and unfortunately, can have unintended negative impacts on quality.

The factory hired a consulting company that proposed a strategy focusing on analyzing frontline employee job behavior to identify the problem. The solution was supported by decades of research and sound reasoning, but the senior managers rejected the solution as simplistic. What happened next has been happening far too much in business these days: the factory managers decided to hire a large consulting company to implement World Class Manufacturing.

Now they will be trying to implement Six Sigma, Lean, and World Class Manufacturing to treat the symptoms but not address the root cause: line workers are not doing some things they should be doing, and they are doing some things they should not be doing. Their behavior is not aligned to produce quality excellence. Many corporations often overlook human behavior aspects and attempt a very complex solution which ends up being much more cumbersome and still does not address the behavioral root cause.

The authors have decades of behavioral performance-improvement experience and we have helped companies become and remain highly competitive and productive. We know that most senior managers are often focused on process and statistical analyses—they don't see that quality issues are caused by something as basic as frontline employee job behavior. This can have a negative and distracting influence on how decisions affecting quality are made. For example, managers can be so convinced that certain practices and problem-solving tools must be used, that their thinking becomes focused on those, and in doing so, they often exclude other possible solutions. When the only tool a person has is a hammer, everything starts to look like a nail. In this book, we will help you build the skills to have a much more flexible and effective approach to workplace management.

What Is a Behavior?

Quality is a result of what frontline employees do or don't do. A reliable method for ensuring quality-focused actions is crucial for success in any competitive marketplace. If your company has struggled with issues similar to those of the component manufacturer, a focus on behavior will help.

The word *behavior* refers to anything you can see someone "do" or hear someone "say." A behavior is physical or verbal and is so specific that it can be counted. The objective of every quality improvement initiative should be to specifically identify activities (behaviors) that a frontline employee can do that will improve quality and then to verify through measurement that this behavior has led to quality improvement.

The fact is that quality efforts have a blind spot, and that blind spot is human behavior. Quality experts have always preached, "It's not the people; it's the process." What they really mean is, "Don't blame the people for defects; fix the process." This advice is good but incomplete. The behavioral approach says, "Fix the process and develop the behaviors expected of the people in the process." A well-designed process must still be implemented by people. Those people need to know exactly which of their behaviors influence the process the most and how well they are performing those behaviors.

Existing quality improvement processes do not often acknowledge that human behavior can cause a large percentage of quality issues. By the time you complete this book, you will have a vastly different understanding about improving quality and productivity in your organization, and such skills will make you a more effective manager. As a manager, you aren't just leading an organization or quality initiatives, or managing the bottom line. In fact, you are leading workplace behavior—whether purposefully or inadvertently. When you can manage behavior with precision, you will then be *effective* at leading your company's quality initiatives, and subsequently improve the bottom line.

To improve quality, we need to improve the defined behaviors that improve quality. To do that, we must address a specific workplace behavioral problem called *behavioral drift*.

Behavioral Drift

Many organizations take the approach that the most effective solution to quality issues is to identify the best way to do a task. The assumption is that if you identify the right way to do a job and provide training and written instructions (in the form of procedures or standard work), then the work will be done correctly. Experience has taught us that this is an incomplete approach. Pressure on frontline employees (external or self-induced) to do more, faster, often drives them to deviate from the prescribed "way they are supposed to do things," leaving out steps and adding their own twist to their jobs. This is called *behavioral drift*.

Why do they do that? Are they bad frontline employees? No, they simply customize their jobs to save time, energy, and avoid immediate discomfort. People have a natural tendency to change their behavior to fit the simplest or easiest way for completing a task. Some frontline employees streamline their approach because it fits within the framework of making a process lean and they don't have a perspective on how their behavior affects the quality of the product down the line. They modify behaviors required to do their job.

One of the major reasons that many frontline employees neglect or avoid behaviors required to sustain a quality effort is because those behaviors add time and effort to their existing job and they don't see the value of those steps. Many of these behaviors are either perceived as too boring or challenging or many frontline employees do not feel comfortable with the requirements necessary to do quality work.

Behavioral Quality Improvement

When the behavioral approach is systematically applied to quality, we call that process *Behavioral Quality Improvement*. Applying the behavioral approach to enhance human performance is not a new phenomenon. Applying the behavioral approach has achieved solid, business-focused results in a wide variety of organizational performance objectives. In each case, changing behavior was the key to achieving the performance objective. Identifying and developing critical-to-quality behaviors is essential to implementing and sustaining any quality initiative and taking quality to a world-class level.

Here are the essential tools of the behavioral approach used in Behavioral Quality Improvement:

1. First, identify the specific, observable, frontline employee behaviors that are affiliated with the causes for poor-quality performance. Most causes of a poor-quality product will include a people factor. You must identify the critical behaviors that frontline employees need to perform to resolve the quality problem being targeted.

2. Next, communicate the complete list of those quality improvement behaviors identified in Step 1 to individuals and workgroups throughout the plant or site. Individuals will then know the critical job functions they need to do to improve quality.

3. Now create a checklist of critical-to-quality behaviors and use it to remind workers that these are priority behaviors. Supervisors and frontline employees will review the checklist regularly.

4. Monitor frontline employee behavior using the checklist. Peers and managers can do the observations of checklist behaviors, and frontline employees can also be trained in self-monitoring.

5. Finally, collect and present data as feedback to the frontline employees and management. Frontline employees set improvement goals and management provides positive recognition for improvement and goal achievement.

This approach becomes a universal formula for frontline employee job success: identify key behaviors linked to quality improvement, provide clear expectations, including checklists, for the frontline employees to ensure they will perform those behaviors as stated and when required, observe the behavior to ensure proper execution, and provide coaching with positive feedback for improvement and goal achievement.

Behavior Quality Improvement deals directly with the issues of behavior change and optimizes a quality improvement plan by identifying the exact behaviors managers and frontline employees need to perform to build the plan into daily work and by ensuring that people receive feedback and recognition for those behaviors. The focus on feedback and recognition for installing the initiative and successfully performing their jobs in new ways is usually not addressed in many quality improvement efforts. Behavioral Quality Improvement provides this essential behavioral component to enhance results.

When the behavioral approach is successfully integrated into organizational performance initiatives, it has achieved remarkable results, such as the following from our consulting experiences:

- Increased customer service **approval rates** from 73 percent to 96 percent

- Saved $30 million in manufacturing **operating costs** within a little over one year

- Produced a **cost savings** of $750,000 in accounting errors within six months

- Achieved a 98 percent **improvement** in accurate codes and commands in software development

- Achieved a 30 percent **improvement** in Manufacturing Department charges/costs in purchasing

- **Reduced fuel consumption** in a trucking company by 10,000 gallons per month and achieved a previously unheard of 83.3 percent operating ratio in that company

- Achieved 99.87 percent **efficiency** in aircraft shipping

- Realized over half a million dollars in **savings** within six months by reducing energy usage in a manufacturing plant

- Moved a manufacturing plant from last to first place in **cost reduction** compared to 99 other manufacturing facilities

- **Reduced a sales backlog** of 20,000 customer contacts to 500 within six months, while servicing a constantly growing customer base

- Moved a department-store chain from last place to first place in **customer service** in an organization with over 300 stores

- **Reduced poor-quality** television screen production from 4 percent to 0.20 percent

- **Reduced selection errors** from 3 percent to less than 0.5 percent in a large distribution center

- **Reduced rework** in auto assembly by 15 percent

Behavioral Quality Improvement is specifically about applying a behavioral approach to critical-to-quality frontline employee behavior. The beauty of this process is that it is easily added to any major quality initiative already being implemented. Drilling down to the specific frontline employee job behavior that is the root cause of the poor-quality outcome will be a powerful addition to your company's quality improvement process.

Why Is Behavioral Quality Improvement Needed?

Quality improvement plans can directly improve an organization's bottom line by reducing the cost of poor quality. The cost of poor quality is typically estimated to be 5 to 30 percent of revenue, or 25 to 40 percent of operating expenses, due to the many visible or hidden costs of poor quality (scrap, rework, repair, returns, complaint handling, warranty costs, and so forth). Thus, implementing quality improvement plans effectively and permanently, the first time, with high employee engagement from the start is essential to organizational success.

Organizations cannot afford to fail to reduce the costs of poor quality, and a quality improvement plan that fails to be embraced by an operating team, or that fails to sustain its original gains after six months or a year, adds to the cost of poor quality. Not only does it fail to reduce the costs of poor quality, but also incurs the cost of the initial implementation (a waste) and the cost of re-implementation (a further waste).

Many of the major quality improvement efforts are having difficulty delivering results. Näslund (2013) highlights some of the problems with such efforts:

> A *Wall Street Journal* article, based on a five-year study, stated that Six Sigma fails to produce

the desired results 60 percent of the time (Chakravorty, 2010). Similarly, Soti et al. (2010) claims that many companies have failed to reap the fruits of the Six Sigma methodology, often taking up valuable organizational resources. A parallel scenario happened for Just-In-Time (JIT) in the 1990s and reports are also starting to occur for Lean (Rosemary and Wempe, 2009; Chakravorty, 2010). A survey by *Industry Week* found that only 2 percent of companies with Lean programs reached their anticipated targets while 74 percent were not making good progress with Lean (Pay, 2008). Farris et al. (2008) claim that most Kaizen descriptions of success are based on anecdotal evidence.

In the beginning of a large quality initiative, management attention and novel activities create interest around executing Lean or Six Sigma processes. Later on, management attention is drawn to other priorities and frontline employee interest seems to drift away.

The major reason for this drift is that most Lean and Six Sigma initiatives do not include ongoing, positive feedback and recognition for improvement and success in implementing critical elements of these processes. Lean and Six Sigma action plans do not include ways to provide behaviorally-specific feedback and recognition to frontline employees for performing the new tasks and behaviors in their newly designed processes.

Quality plans typically focus on analyzing and designing work processes, but not on what people must do to perform well in the new work processes. When quality professionals are busy analyzing and designing work processes, the success of their work process would benefit greatly if they would include behavioral tools in their plans. We encounter these three reasons why they do not:

1. **They see quality initiatives and designs as all-encompassing.** The various quality movements have amassed an extensive array of methodologies. For example, *The Lean Six Sigma Pocket Toolbook* (George, Maxey, Rowlands, and Price, 2004) contains nearly 100 tools and methods. But the huge collection of tools, models, forms, formulas, acronyms, and Japanese names can lull quality practitioners into believing that every element of performance is addressed by one or another of the many quality methodologies. Unfortunately, most quality plans are about analysis and design and fewer are for maintaining performance. None are for defining critical-to-quality behavior. Quality texts note that processes must be sustained and controlled but say little about how to do that.

2. **They leave it to the managers.** Quality initiatives are typically implemented by a special improvement team that studies a problem, designs countermeasures, and hands off the finished plan to the process owner. Many quality guidelines end with a directive to the improvement team that says, in essence, "Hand off the improved process to the process owner who will implement it and build it into standard work." The assumption is that the process owner, managers, and supervisors will know how to encourage the new frontline employee behaviors necessary for successful, sustained process performance. Rather than leave the operating managers to their own devices on how to build a new process into standard work and develop effective management practices, the use of a behavioral approach should be specified.

3. **They count on culture**. All quality movements call for managers to create a culture that institutionalizes quality in the organization. But how does an organization actually create a quality-supportive culture? This is often left up to the executives. The behavioral approach sees culture as the behaviors that an organization maintains through feedback and recognition. Rather than count on a culture created by executives, quality proponents just need executive support to build feedback and recognition for critical-to-quality behaviors into each process.

Why do managers and frontline employees have to learn how to identify critical-to-quality behaviors? Because we tend to think about human performance and discuss it using words that broadly describe what frontline employees should do to improve job performance. We have all heard these directives used by managers to incite the organization to perform better: "Develop a sense of urgency!" "Develop a quality attitude!" "Become more conscientious!" Many of these directives are ambiguous and a matter of perspective. Most importantly, none of these descriptions can be directly observed or counted to provide frontline employees positive feedback and recognition for improvement.

The return-on-investment for using the behavioral approach is much higher than can be achieved with any other organizational initiative. The behavioral approach instills a new mindset into the way we describe successful and unsuccessful frontline employee performance. When managers help instill the specific behaviors they expect, the frontline employees will be more successful in achieving organizational results.

Using the behavioral approach, managers can develop the habit of asking themselves, "What does a frontline employee who has a *dedication to quality* do? How does he or she behave to lead me to say they are dedicated?" If a frontline employee asks, "Boss, what do you want me to do to demonstrate that I am dedicated to quality?" the supervisor or manager will know exactly how to respond.

What Did We Learn in this Chapter?

1. Popular quality improvement initiatives are not consistently achieving the expected improvement results in a large percentage of the companies implementing them.

2. The behavioral approach has a strong track record of success in improving performance.

3. Since the principles that govern human behavior are not understood and applied by quality professionals, behavioral solutions are not included in quality improvement initiatives. The principles of human behavior explain how to

    a. increase the frequency of a positive, productive behavior;

    b. decrease the frequency or stop the performance of an ineffective or incorrect behavior;

    c. encourage someone to perform a new behavior—and sustain that performance.

4. The behavioral approach includes the above and teaches the organization how to break down complex human performance objectives into precise, observable, measurable behaviors.

5. Translating frontline employee quality improvement requirements into observable, measurable behaviors allows managers to provide frontline employees with positive

feedback and recognition for improving and sustaining those behaviors—and creates a positive, motivating culture.

2 DEFINING THE BEHAVIORS THAT DRIVE QUALITY RESULTS

In Chapter 1, several key points help explain why quality improvement initiatives fail to fully achieve expected results and also why they often fail to sustain improvements. The most important factor causing this failure is that none of the popular quality initiatives have a systematic approach to addressing quality-related behavior.

One of the reasons popular quality initiatives do not address behavior stems from the way people typically describe performance. Most people assume that the word *behavior* refers to personality traits, characteristics, or attributes—rather than to specific actions. To many, the phrase "bad attitude" is considered to be the description of a behavior. No existing quality improvement process provides a means for improving a bad attitude.

Unfortunately, the typical way companies try to encourage frontline employees to improve performance is to give them vague objectives like "Take pride in your work!" "Have a can-do attitude!" or "Have a greater sense of urgency!" Managers are also given vague advice by senior managers or consultants, such as "Be a team player," or "Be a people person," or "Embrace change." If you think about it, perhaps you have been told to change the way you do your work, but the suggestions did not give you any clear directions. When someone is told, "Be a self-starter," that person will get a lot more done if the advice is followed by a list of behaviors self-starters perform. While these types of comments are meant to motivate people to improve, they often sound like personal criticism and allegations, and fall short of actually accelerating performance.

Conventional wisdom wrongly assumes that these vague directives are all "behaviors," but they are not. These problem phrases and improvement instructions seem to imply that the frontline employee has some kind of personality issue that acts as an obstacle to optimal performance, but that is very rarely true. What is even more problematic about repeating these platitudes is that when managers blame or label a frontline employee for not having the right attitude, pride, or sense of urgency, it creates a fictional problem that cannot be systematically addressed by managers, supervisors, or by the frontline employee being targeted.

Imagine a work-performance problem is occurring because the frontline employee has not been trained correctly, and the supervisor says, "Well, you better start doing your job!" At that point, the frontline employee likely feels blamed, and the manager may think he or she has helped and takes no further responsibility. The work problem remains unaddressed, and now the confused and frustrated frontline employee may begin to disengage. These types of blame-the-frontline-employee phrases have been handed down since the beginning of the Industrial

Revolution. To managers and supervisors, attempting to work with frontline employees toward improving a "bad attitude" is not possible. It sounds like an affliction the frontline employee was born with. We want to change these problematic old practices, and start having a direct impact on producing effective action in the workplace.

Pinpointing Behavior

Pinpointing in the behavioral approach is a process for turning vague performance objectives into discrete, observable behaviors. We're using the term *pinpointing* to refer to precisely defining work behaviors, so we can measure exactly what kind of effect it has on the process and the product.

The phrases in the last section that talked about attitude, urgency, and pride were not leading to measurable actions. They were poorly defined descriptions of what needed to be done by the frontline employees. Managers have similar problems with the vague and general mandates of quality gurus who often recommend that they "Develop a quality attitude" or "Create a quality culture." Many would say, "Well that's easy, you just *train your frontline employees to be quality oriented*." What specifically does that mean? If you can't be specific, it will mean different things to different people and it will be very difficult to achieve all of the interpretations.

Training is supposed to teach frontline employees how to perform their jobs to a measurable standard. In other words, training aims to instruct people to engage in the right job behaviors; however, it does not ensure they will *consistently perform* those behaviors. For decades, major corporations and industrial managers have relied on training to create improvement and change. Training is certainly a necessary ingredient for conveying the required work behavior, but it does not ensure that behavior will be performed. Nor does retraining for process changes ensure the frontline employee will adopt and consistently follow the new behavior required. Training merely points those trained in the direction of change and improvement.

A manager might ask, "Do you mean it is wrong for me to ask my frontline employees to be committed to quality?" Of course not, as long as you tell them what they need "to do" to demonstrate that commitment. Frontline employees must be informed about the actions and behaviors they need to execute in order to perform quality work.

Some examples of quality-committed behavior would be the following:

- The quality-committed frontline employee would arrive at their workstation a few minutes before their shift begins to evaluate the work area. They want to make sure the previous shift didn't leave a housekeeping problem for them.

- They would check tool placement and make sure that all the tools they need are in the right place.

- They would check their machine and the status of the line to see if product coming down the line is in conformance.

- They would check the bins or shelves where their work material is staged to ensure they had everything they needed and verify that the required documents were filled out correctly by the previous shift.

- Quality-committed frontline employees would inform their supervisor if they saw anything that would negatively affect their performance and/or the product.

- Quality-committed frontline employees would be proactive in anticipating problems that might pose a quality problem, even if it was beyond their area of responsibility.

- If another employee were behind, quality-committed employees would provide assistance if possible.

- If these employees heard any noise from the equipment that indicated a potential problem was developing, they would tell the supervisor.

- If their machine needed recalibration, they would voluntarily relate that information to their supervisor or to maintenance, and inform their supervisor about any substandard material being staged in their bins or on the shelves.

- The quality-committed frontline employee would volunteer any ideas or information that might solve an existing quality problem or improve quality.

- He or she would talk to the supervisor about any issue that might negatively influence quality production.

- The quality-committed frontline employee would volunteer to participate in quality improvement meetings and volunteer improvement ideas whenever possible.

These are examples of a few of the things frontline employees committed to quality would do. So if an employee says to his or her supervisor, "The plant manager was saying we needed to develop a commitment to quality. What does he want us to do?" The supervisor would say, "Well, I can give you a few examples of what I see quality-committed employees do."

1. Arrive at the workstation a few minutes early to do a physical check of the condition of the workstation.

2. Check tool placement for accuracy.

3. Physically evaluate the cleanliness of the area and whether the previous shift has left the area in good order for start-up.

4. Look in the bins and check the shelves to ensure they hold all the materials needed.

5. Look over the equipment to ensure it is ready for start-up.

6. Review required shift documents for accuracy, completeness, and whether the previous operator wrote a comment about anything that might create a problem.

7. Volunteer any information to the supervisor that would help prevent a potential problem on the shift.

8. Volunteer to help frontline employees when they have a problem that will influence quality production.

9. Tell the supervisor or maintenance about any strange noise that indicates a problem developing in the equipment.

10. Inform your supervisor if the equipment needs recalibration.

11. Talk to the supervisor about substandard material being staged in the bins or on the shelves.

12. Volunteer improvement ideas and potential problems.

13. Volunteer to participate in quality improvement meetings and discussions.

These examples show how vague directives from managers , such as "Show commitment!" can be turned into visually observable behaviors that can be counted, and can be used as feedback to help frontline employees manage quality improvement. Such behavioral measures also provide the supervisor with hard data he or she can use for positive feedback.

This example of "Show some commitment!" is similar to other vague instructions that have been used for decades to exhort frontline employees to perform better: "Show some enthusiasm," "Be more conscientious," and "Take things seriously." These phrases, and the ones mentioned in earlier sections are frustrating for the listener. It sounds like they are being criticized for "who they are," rather than "what they do." Behavioral Quality Improvement aims to fix that.

If managers and supervisors understand how to restate such suggestions into the desired, observable behaviors, then frontline employees can have a list of things they can do to meet performance expectations.

Identifying the Specific Behaviors That Cause a Quality Problem

Discovering behavioral causes is like discovering a new vein of gold in a mine you thought was tapped out. It is like doing a behavioral, forensic investigation to discover a single behavior or several behaviors that led to a poor-quality result in the production of a product or service.

Quality problems are often caused not only by what a frontline employee has done, but by what an employee has *not* done. For instance, a frontline employee might not tell the supervisor that the equipment is out of calibration, resulting in product variance. Another employee may fail to warn the foreman that the materials being staged to make the product have some defects. Often frontline employees will see poor-quality product move to their workstation and no one is notified. Consequently, the product with the quality defect is often passed down the line. Failing to perform a behavior that would help eliminate poor-quality product is a common occurrence. Many frontline employees skip a critical-to-quality behavior (task or step) in the job sequence or perform the behaviors in the incorrect sequence.

When this happens, the question always asked is, "Why didn't they notify anyone who might have helped correct and prevent that problem?" Often production speed is a priority. Anything that slows down the line draws negative attention to an operator. The reaction a frontline employee gets from supervision, and even other employees, may include looks of frustration and impatience. Because the frontline employee might not enjoy that kind of negative consequence, he or she might choose not to report defects in the products. In mature quality organizations, frontline employees are encouraged to point out any and all problems that might influence product quality, and doing so leads to positive attention from peers and supervisors.

Consider the following example that occurred in a steel-fabrication facility. For a certain type of high-quality task, welders needed to be formally qualified and tested for performing different types of welds. The qualifications had time limits; each welder had an individual set of welding qualifications, each with its own unique expiration date. On any given day, one welder's qualification might be up-to-date and another welder's qualification might have expired. A quality inspection of a weld included checking the qualifications of the welder. If a welder who was not qualified or whose qualification had expired had performed a weld, the weld was considered defective *even if* the weld itself was physically acceptable. Defective welds had to be removed and re-welded.

The list of welders' qualifications was kept in a hard-copy weld roster.

- One of the critical-to-quality behaviors was that each welder needed to check the weld roster to confirm that his or her qualification for that type of weld was up-to-date *before starting to weld.*

- Another critical-to-quality behavior was that welders check each other's qualifications in the weld roster ("peer checking").

Welders were periodically reminded of the importance of being qualified for each type weld. But qualification problems— and thus defects and rework—sometimes occurred. *Why didn't welders just check the weld roster?* Some managers complained that welders were lazy or sloppy or had a poor work ethic. But from a behavioral perspective there was no reason to assume the frontline employees were any of those things.

> *At the core of these behavioral issues was that welders who had worked in other environments with less-rigorous quality standards were not used to checking qualifications prior to work. These welders were used to focusing on the act of welding, not on reviewing paperwork. It took extra effort to look in the weld roster. Other welders trusted their memories from the last time they checked. The real issue in this situation was that there was no observation-and-feedback system to ensure the frontline employees complied with the expectations.*

Frontline employees often perform a job behavior differently than specified by the job standard. To save time, energy, and real or perceived discomfort, sometimes frontline employees deviate from the formal procedure. The product variations created by this behavioral variation are not caught until further down the manufacturing line, or when discovered by a customer.

Frontline employees not meeting the job expectations can cause numerous quality problems. There are many reasons this could occur. Sometimes this is a training problem or a misunderstanding on their part. Or, they have partially understood and put their own spin on the way a task or step is performed because they did not want to appear stupid by asking for help. These point to a behavioral problem. "Doing it the wrong way," often referred to as a "failure to follow procedure" is one of the most common causes of poor-quality performance. Poor-quality performance leads to product-line rejection and customer returns.

In summary, frontline employees influence poor-quality production when they

1. fail to do or say something that would prevent poor quality;

2. change one or more job behaviors;

3. fail to perform expected job behaviors;

4. perform job behaviors incorrectly.

In most cases, specific behaviors a frontline employee does or fails to do are fairly easy to discover, either by questioning or direct observation. In every workgroup, several behaviors are critical to ensuring product quality. Departments or workgroups rarely pinpoint those behaviors. Posting graphs of behavioral measures on a board for everyone to see is one means of focusing everyone on essential behaviors to attend to for that week, month, or permanently. Discussions about critical-to-quality behaviors are more instructive and productive than instructing frontline employees to "Make sure you do this!"

Most groups can meet for an hour, identify the critical-to-quality behaviors, and immediately use them to create a behavior checklist that each frontline employee can use to improve the behaviors that address the problem.

This immediacy is absent from existing quality cause analyses. A Behavioral Quality Improvement approach can save frontline employee problem-solving time off the job, solve problems faster, and often eliminate the need for more expensive engineering solutions. Also, it saves money compared to lengthy quality training processes like Six Sigma and Lean. The cost for implementing Behavioral Quality Improvement can be one-tenth the cost of other quality-improvement processes (and yields much greater returns).

An additional benefit is that Behavioral Quality Improvement does not conflict with other engineering and statistical methods. Behavioral Quality Improvement can help enhance, rejuvenate, and sustain existing quality processes.

What Did We Learn in this Chapter?

1. Personality traits, characteristics, or attributes are not behaviors. To change behavior, it is important to translate phrases that refer to traits or labels, like "Be a self-starter," into behaviors (observable actions) that the person can actually do.

2. *Pinpointing* is a process of turning vague performance objectives into discrete, observable behaviors. Pinpointing refers to precisely defining work behaviors that can be observed and counted.

3. Once key work behaviors are pinpointed, one can observe whether those behaviors are occurring. Quality results can be

affected by frontline employee behaviors like

a. failing to do or say something that would prevent poor quality;

b. changing one or more job behaviors in the quality process;

c. failing to perform expected job behaviors;

d. performing job behaviors incorrectly.

3 THE QUALITY ACTION TEAM: FIRST STEPS

One of the first steps of Behavioral Quality Improvement is to identify a dedicated team of people who will be responsible for guiding its implementation. A Quality Action Team is always formed at the beginning of every Behavioral Quality Improvement implementation. It is essential that the team members are interested and enthusiastic about promoting quality improvement. If the right people are selected for that team, they will infuse other frontline employees with enthusiasm and positive expectations for the process. Each Quality Action Team member should feel comfortable working with others to identify problems and implement solutions.

Our experience indicates that any systematic organizational quality-improvement effort must have manager support and involvement to succeed and sustain. Manager *support* is frequently mentioned as vital in quality-improvement initiatives; yet a clear definition of *support* is never presented. What managers are expected "to do" to demonstrate support is not precisely described. The Quality Action Team will solve this problem in two ways. First, at least one person on the Quality Action Team will be an upper-level manager with solid knowledge of organizational resources and the process for creating support for change at the senior-management level. Second, the Quality Action Team will work with all levels of management to identify and commit to perform the specific behaviors required of managers to visibly demonstrate support and involvement.

Selecting the Quality Action Team

Involving frontline employees in an organizational quality-improvement process increases frontline employee buy-in and support. The Quality Action Team will encourage frontline employee participation by selecting its members from a cross section of departments, workgroups, and management levels. The mix of workplace representation is carefully selected to ensure the Quality Action Team has credibility with frontline employees.

An important question is, "Who selects the members of the Quality Action Team?" The answer is the person who initiates an implementation of Behavioral Quality Improvement at a site would be the first member; then he or she will obtain management authority to put the team together. This initiating, frontline employee may be someone already implementing an existing quality initiative and who, after reading this book, recognizes the benefits of adding behavioral solutions to achieve better sustained results. Or the Quality Action Team leader may see the value of discovering behavioral causes for problems and influencing the frontline employees' behaviors that lead to higher quality.

If a frontline supervisor recognizes the value of the concepts presented here, he or she can develop internal interest by passing the book around and initiating dialogs with peers and decision makers. The supervisor could also pass the book to an existing quality champion or senior manager with a history of interest in quality improvement.

If a senior-level manager reads this book, he or she could ask other managers to read the book and develop a consensus to move forward. Managers might then select as the first Quality Action Team member someone who would be a champion for quality improvement and who would work with the managers to select additional team members to create the positive team dynamics required to initiate, implement, and sustain Behavioral Quality Improvement across the site. The Quality Action Team should have a cross section of management and frontline employees from various functions.

The Quality Action Team size will be determined by the size of the site. The number of members varies but our experience would caution having over 10 members. A six- to eight-member team is usually effective. If you have an extremely large plant with many functional areas, consider creating an additional Quality Action Team. The number of Quality Action Teams is not as important as the fact that two or more Quality Action Teams need to communicate with each other and share information and practices. Each group should share its important learnings. When one Quality Action Team solves a quality problem, the other groups should have access to the details.

Other factors to consider in selecting Quality Action Team members include the following:

- Good communications skills, especially the ability to have logical discussions, express clear opinions, listen to others, and encourage positive contributions

- Knowledge of existing quality initiatives and quality-improvement practices

- Solid working knowledge of the production process and departmental functions

- Interest in promoting positive change and making a difference in quality

- Willingness to speak in front of peers and managers

- Natural leadership and the ability to work effectively within a high-performing team

- Have credibility among peers and management

It is not necessary for a candidate to have all these traits, but this list provides some guidance in deciding which frontline employees to ask to join the team. Candidates who are interested in quality improvement and enjoy team problem solving will more than likely volunteer when you ask. Our experience in forming committees for behavior-based interventions is that volunteer members are typically more enthusiastic and productive than those who have been assigned.

Chartering the Quality Action Team

Once the members have been selected, the Quality Action Team will establish ground rules for meeting and produce an agreement about the team's purpose and objectives. If the Quality Action Team members have prior experience with group problem solving, they may not have to spend much time on establishing rules of order. However, certain principles should be made clear, such as the voting process to make decisions, raising hands to initiate comments or questions, and allowing others to speak without interruption. Also, the team can briefly discuss how team idea-building and brainstorming produce innovation, how respectful language avoids contentious discussions, and so forth. Additional rules of order can be established as the team begins to function. New rules may be needed to maintain order and keep the focus on identifying and solving quality problems with the behavioral approach.

At the first meeting, the Quality Action Team should discuss its purpose and goals. The purpose and goals should be written clearly and stated using specific terms. The team can borrow from the list below.

Purpose: The purpose of the Quality Action Team includes the following:

- Implement Behavioral Quality Improvement at the site.

- Apply the behavioral approach to existing quality problems.

- Enhance the effectiveness of existing quality initiatives by strengthening the problem-solving process.

- Identify new quality-improvement opportunities and apply the behavioral approach.

Process: To achieve our purpose, the Quality Action Team will do the following:

- Identify the behaviors that cause quality problems and the frontline employee behaviors that ensure high-quality results by analyzing quality data and interviewing managers, frontline employees, and stakeholders.

- Identify any factors in the work environment that are positively or negatively influencing quality performance.

- Create a checklist of critical-to-quality behaviors needed to solve the quality problem.

- Select from volunteer frontline employees who are trained to observe individuals and workgroups, present them with positive feedback for performing critical-to-quality behaviors, and relate any concerns they may have about frontline employee performance. They will ask the frontline employee if there is anything that would help him or her by removing a barrier or make it easier to perform quality work.

- Use that checklist as the basis for a tracking system that will produce data about the frequency of the critical-to-quality behaviors that will solve the problem.

- Maintain visible data graphs on each project and post the graphs.

- Track behavioral data and compare to existing quality results data.

- Develop goals for improvement in the critical-to-quality behaviors over time.

- Create celebration plans that will reward frontline employees for meeting those goals.

- Review the quality-improvement methods currently being used and identify opportunities where the behavioral approach will improve their effectiveness.

- Determine whether any frontline employees need additional training on how to perform the critical-to-quality behaviors, and assist in the development of that training.

- Study Behavioral Quality Conversations and prepare a training event to teach all levels of management how to perform them in everyday work conversations and meetings. (See Chapter 6.)

- Teach managers and supervisors how to have Behavioral Quality Conversations in which they collect information about progress, identify barriers, and discover any resources the frontline employees need to perform better.

- Prepare a roadmap for implementing Behavioral Quality Improvement at the site, prepare a prioritized list of existing quality problems, and present this plan to senior management.

- Launch Behavioral Quality Improvement by communicating to the workforce what the Quality Action Team will be doing and emphasize that the Quality Action Team seek positive solutions and avoid assigning blame.

The Quality Action Team's work results in the following outcomes:

- An approved plan for building and sustaining the critical-to-quality behaviors essential for high-quality results

- The discovery of new quality-improvement opportunities

- The removal of barriers and the revision of systems issues that limit quality performance

- Posted feedback and evidence of improvement in quality issues

- Tracked and communicated improvements in quality results

Prioritizing and Selecting Quality Problems

After the Quality Action Team has identified its purpose and goals, you need to select an existing quality problem to address. Your company may have a long list of quality problems. Many factors will determine the quality problem you choose for your first target. Obviously, if a quality problem is causing catastrophic or dangerous outcomes, then it requires the most immediate attention. Quality issues that are threatening the financial well-being of the organization move higher on the list.

If your company is not dealing with critical factors such as these, there are a few other considerations. One issue for the Quality Action Team to think about is if they should swing for the fences with a big issue, or get on base with a smaller issue. Sometimes a newly formed Quality Action Team that has never used Behavioral Quality Improvement before decides to simply practice using the behavioral approach on a smaller quality issue, and makes sure that the first time leads to a "win." In other words, the Team should consider selecting a target that may be easy to address. This allows the team to gain experience with the behavioral approach before working on more significant issues that may be more difficult and more complex.

Identifying Critical-to-Quality Behaviors

Once the Quality Action Team has prioritized a list of quality problems in the order in which they will be solved, the next task is to identify the critical-to-quality behaviors associated with the first quality problem. Identifying these behaviors provides the foundation for all of the Quality Action Team's subsequent work.

The Quality Action Team brainstorms which groups of performers have the greatest impact on the quality result. Then for each group identified, the Quality Action Team members ask themselves, "What observable behavior, or series of behaviors, could these performers do to reduce or eliminate defects?" It helps to ask the question in several different ways: "What results-driving actions need to happen more often, more quickly, or better? What are the big things that people need to do that will make the difference in quality on this particular problem? What behavior do we want to make sure that every frontline employee influencing this quality problem will do consistently? Is there a behavior the performer should stop doing or substitute with a more effective behavior?" In addition to asking each other, the Quality Action Team members can ask the frontline employees themselves about critical-to-quality behaviors. Sometimes frontline employees who work in a process every day know which behaviors are critical to quality, but no one has asked them.

Let's take a look at an example where the frontline employees at an organization were a great source of information on critical-to-quality behaviors. Our consultant was asked by a company that makes vaccines to help improve the quality of vaccine production. The company made vaccines that were used by all chicken-raising companies and by all individual chicken ranchers. The vaccine was used to eliminate chicken influenza. The process for making the vaccines was conducted in a sterile laboratory where the fluid around a fertilized egg embryo was injected with the virus. After several days, the fluid was extracted and used as a flu vaccine. The company was getting a 92 percent yield of quality vaccine in their production process. Each percentage point improvement in quality yield equaled $100,000 per week in increased revenue for the company.

The consultant visited the laboratory and met with a group of plant supervisors to find out what the laboratory workers could do to improve quality and increase yield. During a long morning meeting in a boardroom, the supervisors admitted that they did not know how to increase the yield, and the discussion was getting nowhere. During a break in the meeting, the consultant requested that the laboratory supervisor contact his lead laboratory person and tell her to ask the other workers the question, "Can you guys come up with three or more things that you could do to improve the quality of the vaccine yield?" He said it would be easy to make that call and promptly did so.

After the break, the consultant asked the laboratory supervisor how the lab frontline employees responded. The supervisor said they had brainstormed and identified five critical behaviors that would increase quality. The supervisors were astounded to discover that just asking the people who did the work could so easily solve the problem, even though management could not solve it for months. Within one month, yield quality had increased from 92 percent to 97 percent, increasing company revenue by $500,000 *per week*!

In the laboratory example, the supervisors did not know the behaviors needed to improve quality; however, there are times when managers do know exactly what frontline employees should do to improve quality, and are frustrated that only some frontline employees engage in those behaviors. Downstream-production workgroups who receive product that is off-quality often refer to the experience as "pass the trash." This group often knows which behaviors make the difference in producing high-quality work, but is seldom asked to provide a list of those behaviors. Usually, when asked, they are highly motivated to describe the behaviors not being performed or being performed incorrectly.

The Quality Action Team can also invite subject-matter experts to a meeting to serve as a resource in helping identify the cause of a behavioral, quality problem. The engineers who designed the work process, the trainers who teach the relevant job skills, or the quality inspectors who check the finished work often know exactly which behaviors are essential for frontline employees to perform to achieve quality.

If necessary, the Quality Action Team can assemble a group of frontline employees, managers, or customers and ask them to brainstorm critical-to-quality behaviors. List the behaviors and then have the group discuss each behavior and rate it in terms of its importance. The end product should be a prioritized list of several critical-to-quality behaviors frontline employees can change to improve quality results.

Another approach for identifying critical-to-quality behaviors is for a Quality Action Team member to observe the best performing individuals or teams in action, and see exactly what they do differently to achieve quality. For example, in a steel fabrication facility, observation of the best welding team showed that the foremen and welders used gauges and other inspection tools to self-inspect their welds before calling for the official review by a quality-control inspector. The production team's self-inspection helped them improve the quality of the work and increased the likelihood that the welds passed inspection, saving time and rework.

Identifying the Factors That Influence Critical-to-Quality Behaviors

Once the Quality Action Team has identified the critical-to-quality behaviors, the next step is to identify the factors that influence those behaviors. The team will look for environmental factors in the workplace that prompt or support the wrong behavior or fail to bring out the right behavior from frontline employees. Such factors might include, for example, old equipment, outdated software, inconvenient placement of tools, or poor communication. The Quality Action Team then develops action plans to address those factors.

Two kinds of factors that influence critical-to-quality behaviors are

1. systems factors;

2. communication factors.

Systems factors. Systems factors are built-in elements of the work process, workplace environment, or organization systems, such as workflow, equipment, materials, procedures, training, and so forth that make it difficult to perform the right behavior or easier to perform the wrong behavior.

The Quality Action Team will look for built-in causes of suboptimal behavior such as these:

1. The workflow can be improved.

2. Procedures are not clear.

3. The ergonomics of the work tasks can be improved.

4. The pace of production or work time is out of sync with tasks.

5. Tools are difficult to use or not available.

6. Equipment is not capable or maintained.

7. Materials are not available when needed or difficult to work with.

8. Hardcopy or digital information is not available.

9. Frontline employees are not trained or need additional training.

10. There are no signs, visual reminders, or job aids prompting the desired behavior.

For example, a large multinational retail store had a quality problem in one of their distribution centers. Incorrect merchandise was being shipped to customers. This was having a negative effect on the brand's customer base and costing a considerable amount of wasted time in return processing and reshipping. The first assumption was that the "pickers" who pulled the merchandise off of the warehouse risers were misreading the pick order, which is a sheet with all the merchandise they are to load on a pallet and stage in the outgoing freight area.

Upon further investigation, a Quality Action Team discovered that one major cause of this problem was that the shifts were understaffed. The number of pickers was below how many were needed to do all of the work that was required each day. The existing staff had more work than they could handle and had to work at an extremely fast pace that inevitably forced errors to occur.

The Quality Action Team then realized the shifts were shorthanded, and dug deeper to determine why they were so understaffed. Was Human Resources not hiring at a pace necessary to populate the pick staff? The consultant interviewed the supervisors who said that the right number of people were being hired, but an excessive number dropped out of training before they even started work.

The Quality Action Team then interviewed people who had dropped out of training and trainees still in the training program. That was when the consultant discovered the real problem: the training was ineffective. Trainees were asked to do things they did not have sufficient knowledge to do and they were making errors. The trainees who dropped out did so because they thought they were failing and that the work was going to be too difficult for them.

With so many trainees dropping out of the training, the company never had the number of pick staff necessary to do the work. The training staff needed to redevelop their sequence of lessons, the training content, and become more encouraging to new trainees. So in this case, eliminating the critical-to-quality behavior that produced errors meant drilling down into the work environment like a detective.

Communication factors. Communication factors are the interactions and conversations that should be happening to strengthen the right behaviors. Frontline employees should be performing in a safe, feedback-rich environment that prompts and notices the critical-to-quality behaviors.

The Quality Action Team will look for these causes of the critical-to-quality behaviors and ensure that they are occurring:

1. The importance of performing the critical-to-quality behavior has been explained and emphasized.

2. Pre-shift and post-shift meetings address the performance of critical-to-quality behaviors.

3. Critical-to-quality behaviors are observed and data are collected.

4. Supervisors have individual and team conversations in which they listen to frontline employees about barriers to doing high-quality work.

5. Managers at all levels have conversations with direct reports that include data-based feedback about critical-to-quality behavior.

6. Data-based, graphical feedback is posted so that frontline employees "know their score" related to critical-to-quality behaviors.

7. Managers at all levels pay attention to direct reports when behaviors and results improve.

8. Observation and positive feedback are built into action plans, procedures, and standard work.

9. Frontline employees use checklists to observe their own behavior.

10. Feedback conversations show the impact of critical-to-quality behaviors on quality results.

The key communication factor is data-based feedback about critical-to-quality behavior. If there is no feedback for performing a critical-to-quality behavior, the behavior will not sustain. But if you can provide positive feedback (meaning the person receiving the feedback deems it positive) when the frontline employee is performing the critical-to-quality behavior, then you will strengthen the behavior.

The Quality Action Team identifies systems and communication factors that influence the critical-to-quality behavior and takes the appropriate action to ensure that systems and communication support and strengthen critical-to-quality behaviors. That is what Behavioral Quality Improvement is all about!

What Did We Learn in this Chapter?

1. A Quality Action Team is always formed at the beginning of every Behavioral Quality Improvement implementation.

2. A six- to eight-member team is usually effective.

3. Quality Action Team members should have good communications skills, knowledge of existing quality initiatives, knowledge of the production process and departmental functions, interest in improving quality, natural

leadership, ability to work effectively on a team, and credibility among peers and management.

4. The Quality Action Team prioritizes quality problems, identifies the critical-to-quality behaviors that will resolve those problems, and creates checklists for the observation of the critical-to-quality behaviors.

5. The Quality Action Team teaches observers how to observe critical-to-quality behaviors and how to provide effective feedback to the performers.

6. The Quality Action Team monitors all aspects of the Behavioral Quality Improvement process.

4 CREATING EFFECTIVE BEHAVIOR CHECKLISTS

Checklists are effective tools for supporting performance in almost any setting, especially the workplace. Using checklists helps ensure performance excellence in a wide range of industries. Surgeons, nurses, pilots, construction supervisors— anyone who wants to ensure that important behaviors are performed correctly—are putting together checklists.

Unfortunately, organizations have a tendency to use checklists to find out who is to blame for poor quality. The word *audit* is typically associated with checklists that look for errors and problems. Fortunately, not all checklists have focused exclusively on blaming when errors are found, and when used constructively, they have a significant impact on optimizing work behaviors. Well-developed checklists that aim to improve quality describe exactly the correct behaviors the performer should complete to ensure solid outcomes.

Effective Checklists List Specific Behaviors

The purpose of using checklists in the Behavioral Quality Improvement approach is not to audit people's actions to see if they did something incorrectly. Behavioral Quality Improvement is more interested in using checklists as a guide for the frontline employee to ensure that they do not skip critical-to-quality behaviors or do them out of order. The checklist focuses on what to do, not just what was not done. Because you are developing a process for encouraging correct behaviors and sequences, you must utilize specific pinpoints when generating checklists.

Before looking at a few examples of good checklists, let's look at how checklists can cause inefficient behavior or problems. One particular company was trying to improve workplace productivity by using checklists. They even created a checklist for the corporate managers. Now, it isn't very often that organizations ask managers to follow a checklist, even though it is a good idea. The problem with most management checklists is that they seldom describe specific behaviors. Even the descriptions of manager performance objectives are often vague.

Figure 1 shows a manager self-evaluation checklist on "Providing Organizational Direction." The purpose of the checklist is to provide the manager with a few criteria related to providing direction to the organization. Think about what you learned in Chapter 2 about pinpointing, and then notice how misguided this checklist is. If you look at the performance requirements, the key phrases are extremely vague. No actions are truly specified. The manager needs to have pinpointed behaviors that describe specifically how to activate the vague instructions of *help, encourage, foster,* and *communicate.*

Providing Organizational Direction	
Behaviors	**Check**
1	Help others recognize the value of their contributions to the organization	
2	Ensure that everyone in the work unit understands the organization's vision and strategy	
3	In direct reports, foster a sense of personal responsibility for the organization's success	
4	Make the organization's vision and strategy a part of regular conversations with the work unit	
5	Communicate the organization's vision and strategy in ways that others find compelling	

Figure 1. A manager self-evaluation checklist on providing organizational direction

This checklist is an example of how directions, instructions, and performance objectives leave frontline employees—even managers—totally confused about what they are supposed to be doing to be successful. Checklists are used for many other aspects of work at a job site. They can direct step-by-step daily procedures for manufacturing, or describe maintenance procedures that are scheduled every six months. In either case, they are important for keeping critical-to-quality behaviors on track and in sequence.

Checklists can also help reduce injury and incidents. Safety professionals often create a job-hazard analysis in checklist form to describe how to do a job correctly and avoid incidents. In dynamic environments, hazardous tasks are managed with one or more preparation checklists. For example, preventive safety

Confined Space Entry Procedure Checklist		
	Steps	**Check**
1	Isolate the space from all hazards	
1a	Remove unauthorized personnel from entry site	
1b	LOTO (Lockout/Tagout)	
1c	Blocking inlets, etc.	
2	Ventilate the space (if required)	
3	Fill out the Entry Permit	
4	Evaluate the space	
5	Test the atmosphere	
5a	Enter atmosphere readings on the permit	
5b	Place the completed permit at the confined space	
6	Enter the space and proceed with work	
6a	Is Supervisor available?	
6b	Attendant at the entry site	
6c	Harness	
6d	Required personal protective equipment (PPE)	
6e	Retest atmosphere as needed/required	
7	When the job is done:	
7a	Remove all personnel, tool, debris from space	
7b	Close the space	
7c	Cancel the permit	
7d	Review job with supervisor (hazards, etc.)	
8	File the completed and closed permit	

Figure 2. A confined space entry safety procedure checklist

procedures for Confined Space Entry work are placed on a checklist. Usually an employee designated as the "attendant" is suitably trained and responsible for maintaining a watch over those entering the confined space, for maintaining communications with those inside the space, and for initiating emergency procedures in the event of an incident occurring.

The Confined Space Entry Procedure Checklist in Figure 2 is an example of a checklist with some items that are not pinpointed. For example, Item "1b LOTO (lockout/tagout)" does explain exactly what an observer looks for to ensure that the appropriate equipment is de-energized and locked out. This checklist could be dangerous because many items are vague and don't describe what needs to be done. The Quality Action Team would be able to make this list much more effective. Notice how some of the behaviors on the checklist are unclear and leave a large margin of interpretation about the behavior to be performed.

Consider, for instance, checklist item #5—Test the atmosphere. To ensure that the atmosphere is tested properly, the phrase "Test the atmosphere," should be broken down into the specific behaviors required to complete that task properly. To put this task in perspective, the Michigan Occupational Safety and Health Administration has a 24-page document entitled "Guidelines for Developing a Permit Required Confined Space Entry Written Program." Certain tasks, especially when dealing with dynamic and hazardous environments, require specific and robust checklists. Imagine if your company treated quality with the same dedication.

The Michigan Occupational Safety and Health Administration document includes many lists of behaviors that need to be performed by the employer, the supervisor, the attendant, and the frontline employees who will work in the confined space. A small section refers to evaluating the atmosphere:

Evaluate confined space conditions as follows:

1. *Before entry, test conditions in the permit space to determine if acceptable entry conditions exist; if necessary, continuously monitor entry conditions where entrants are working.*

2. *Test or monitor the permit space as necessary to ensure entry conditions are maintained.*

3. *When testing for atmospheric hazards, test first for oxygen, then for combustible gases and vapors and then for toxic substances.*

4. *Provide entrants the opportunity to observe any pre-entry or subsequent testing or monitoring of permit spaces.*

5. *Reevaluate the permit space when requested to do so by an entrant.*

6. *Immediately provide each entrant with the results of any testing conducted.*

Comparing the two checklists demonstrates the benefits of pinpointing the behaviors on the checklist quite specifically. The Quality Action Team's task is to ensure that any checklist of critical-to-quality behaviors is written with a high level of clarity. Clarity and specificity will guarantee that all pinpoints on the checklist can be performed as required. The challenge is often to ensure that the checklist has the right amount of detail without becoming too long to serve as a useful tool.

When to Use Critical-to-Quality Checklists

In which situations can critical-to-quality checklists be helpful? The simple answer is *whenever behavior is essential to quality and those behaviors are not now done consistently and correctly by all performers.* Below are some specific situations in which checklists are particularly effective:

- **When processes require multiple behaviors**. When a process requires a set or series of behaviors, a checklist can ensure that frontline employees do not skip over critical-to-quality behaviors.

- **When behavior must be consistent across frontline employees, teams, or shifts**. One of the most frustrating quality challenges is consistency of behavior. The answer to the question "Is everyone doing what they need to do to ensure quality?" is often, "Some are; some aren't," or "It depends on where you look." In these cases, a checklist can help produce consistent performance by specifying a uniform set of behaviors for all frontline employees.

- **When a process changes**. Quality problems are often created when a product is redesigned and new equipment has to be added or old equipment customized. Frontline employees then have to do their jobs differently to ensure quality. The need for new work behavior usually leads to higher error rates because frontline employees are used to doing things the old way. Checklists specify the essential new behaviors that a new process requires.

- **When new frontline employees join a work process**. New frontline employees introduce a high probability for behavioral error into a process. Their lack of familiarity with the work skills, slower work pace, and inexperience when dealing with challenges creates an obstacle for fluid and reliable quality outcomes. Checklists instantly orient new frontline employees to the behaviors they should perform, help them become familiar with the process, and can even help them know what to do in the case of a rare mishap on the line (rather than counting on trial and error to help them become more experienced). Checklists also allow experienced frontline employees to better train new frontline employees on the job.

- **When a cycle of constant redirecting and retraining appears.** Sometimes managers find themselves repeatedly directing and urging frontline employees to perform better, and scheduling training again and again. When a never-ending cycle of substandard behavior/redirecting/retraining appears, a behavior checklist is the solution. Behavior checklists set the standard for performance and allow feedback on actual behavior.

- **When the behaviors are performed intermittently.** If frontline employees do not perform tasks on a regular basis, they may not recall the proper steps for executing the action. Annual maintenance tasks are at risk for quality issues if a checklist is not used. The maintenance frontline employee will perform the critical-to-quality actions if he or she does not have to rely on memory from the last time this work was performed. The same issue is present with rare emergencies. Of course it is critical to respond immediately to an emergency, which is why we train people to be very fluent in how to respond. When serious incidents occur, such as an oil spill or fire in the factory, it is a great idea to have the manager use a checklist for directing the frontline employees and the first responders.

Production Start-Work Checklist		
	Order of Steps	**Check**
1	Foreman gets written work instructions based on direction from Supervisor	
2	Foreman conducts pre-job brief and job safety analysis meeting with crew	
3	Foreman reviews weld logs and checks status of welds (fit tacks, weld-outs, etc.)	
4	Foreman gets direction on work sequences to work on based on written work instructions and drawing	
5	Foreman reviews the welding procedure specification for accuracy	
6	Foreman reviews weld log to verify prior work (complete, accurate, signed off) and weld roster to choose a qualified welder	
7	Foreman assigns welder and issues weld-wire ticket (Welders peer-check for accuracy)	
8	Welder checks out weld wire from storeroom	
9	Welder returns and sets up machine	
10	Per the Foreman's instruction, Welder pre-heats as needed and then begins welding	
11	Foreman checks job frequently	
12	Welder checks completed weld, then Foreman checks weld, calls Quality Control for inspection	

Figure 3. A production start-work checklist showing the behavioral steps that must be followed in the right order

Short and Lengthy Critical-to-Quality Checklists

Critical quality checklists will vary in length depending on the number of behaviors causing the quality problem. Sometimes the

Quality Action Team will discover quality problems are related to only three to five critical-to-quality behaviors. But sometimes the Quality Action Team will identify 10 or more behaviors that need to be precisely performed to ensure quality. When errors are occurring across a wide range of behaviors, a longer list will be required to ensure a better quality process.

The checklist in Figure 3 is an example of a situation in which a set of behavioral steps must be followed in the right order to ensure quality. In this steel fabrication facility, first-time quality requires that welders must follow precise instructions on procedures, materials, welder qualifications, documentation, and so forth. To achieve quality, the production team must follow the exact order of the steps required to start work at the beginning of a shift. The production team uses the checklist to ensure that no start-up behaviors are skipped. In turn, completion of this checklist is itself a quality behavior that the team has committed to perform 100 percent of the time. This checklist also demonstrates an example in which a foreman and a frontline employee are working as a team to improve quality.

Combining Critical-to-Quality Behaviors and Safety Behavior in a Checklist

The checklist in Figure 4 comes from an equipment-manufacturing plant where we implemented the Behavioral Quality Improvement approach. This is an example of a shorter checklist (filled out by an operator) that includes a safety-related behavior as well as critical-to-quality behaviors. Personal Protective Equipment (PPE) is added to this example because "putting on PPE prior to starting work" was a set of behaviors not being performed regularly at the plant, and injuries were occurring.

Manufacturing Quality Checklist		
	Behaviors	**Check**
1	Operator wears basic PPE consisting of safety glasses, full earplugs, and safety shoes throughout the shift	
2	Operator updates inspection records, within the times specified on the inspection instruction sheet	
3	Operator confirms he or she knows how to perform all the measurements required on the Inspection Sheet	
4	Operator fills in the Self-Maintenance Sheet according to the frequency requested	
5	Operator confirms knowledge of how to perform all the self-maintenance required by the Self-Maintenance Sheet	

Figure 4. Checklist showing both safety-related behavior and critical-to-quality behaviors

Selecting the Most Critical-to-Quality Behaviors

The checklist in Figure 5 is an example taken from a successful airline. Airlines have many quality-related criteria to ensure that passengers' flying experience is world class. Each segment of airline service is responsible for customer-service behaviors. The frontline employees at the ticket counters, gate agents, and flight attendants interface with passengers constantly, and every major airline strives to constantly improve the quality of customer service.

Cabin-cleaning crews have a very long checklist of behaviors to perform, because passenger satisfaction is influenced by the

	Cabin Appearance Quality Checklist	
	Main Cabin	**Check**
1	Inspect overhead bin doors for cleanliness and fingerprints	
2	Remove trash and dust from bin interior	
3	Lift armrests and clean underneath; remove any scuff marks	
4	Check armrest and ensure it is clean and free of scuff marks	
5	Inspect in-flight entertainment screen and remove fingerprints, smudges, and streaks	
6	Open tray tables and remove any marks or stains	
7	Remove any smudges from sidewall, window, and window shade	
8	Inspect white seatbacks; clear of scuff marks	
9	Check seat pocket for safety card, red guide, and airsickness bag and stock if necessary	
10	Clean stains and crumbs from seats	
11	Vacuum rug areas	
12	Remove all trash from between seats, on seats, and in seat pockets	

Figure 5. Checklist of behaviors for airline cabin appearance quality

cleanliness of the cabin and the immediate environment surrounding their seats.

In this instance, our consultant analyzed the long list, and through interviews with management, employees, and passengers, identified the critical-to-quality behaviors that were not being performed satisfactorily. Figure 5 is the long list of pinpointed behaviors for cleaning and inspecting the main cabin.

After reviewing passenger surveys, the consultant identified the five critical-to-quality behaviors from the list above:

1. Open tray tables and remove any marks or stains.

2. Remove smudges from sidewall, window, and window shade.

3. Clean stains and crumbs from seats.

4. Vacuum rug areas.

5. Remove all trash between seats, on seats, and in seat pockets.

Sorting through all the behaviors that a frontline employee may do to select the few behaviors linked to solving a specific quality problem is the key function that Behavioral Quality Improvement introduces into organizational quality initiatives. On some checklists, every listed item is important; selecting one or two is impossible. In a frontline employee's job, there are hundreds of behaviors, but 95 percent of the time only a few can be directly linked to the quality problem.

In this chapter, a wide variety of critical-to-quality checklist issues were discussed. These various examples will help the Quality Action Team adapt checklists to different situations in their facility. The first part of this book has focused on how to identify critical-to-quality behaviors and create checklists that enable employees to be appropriately observed, perform self-checks, and solve quality problems along with the Quality Action Team.

To provide meaningful feedback to a frontline employee, a measurement system must be developed using the checklist data. These data will also be important to share with workgroups and even the plant as a whole in order to see how well the organization is meeting the quality benchmarks. Chapters 5 and 6 will show how to create meaningful measures and how to reward significant accomplishments in performing critical-to-quality behaviors.

What Did We Learn in this Chapter?

1. Checklists are lists of important actions that must be performed to ensure a performance outcome.

2. Checklist items must be very specific to ensure they are performed exactly as required.

3. Critical-to-quality checklists are composed of the specific behaviors that are essential to a quality result.

4. Safe behaviors and critical-to-quality behaviors can be incorporated into one checklist.

5. Checklists provide quantitative information that allows performers to receive positive feedback and information for improvement.

5 COLLECTING AND ANALYZING BEHAVIORAL DATA

Once the Quality Action Team has identified critical-to-quality behaviors and created behavior checklists, the next task is to collect data about how often these critical-to-quality behaviors are actually occurring.

One of our consultants was fortunate enough to be hired by a beer brewery. While he was teaching a workshop to a group of frontline supervisors, he described what a behavior was and the fact that it is visible or auditory and can be counted.

At the end of that discussion, the consultant called for a 15-minute break and was about to leave when a supervisor named Carl raised his hand. The consultant said, "Yes Carl?" Carl said, "Did you know that in the last 30 minutes you moved your hands in and out of your front pockets 35 times?" The consultant was astounded that the supervisor had such a good example of counting behavior—even at his expense.

He said, "That's great, Carl. You learned how to count a visible behavior very quickly." Carl said, "And you used the verbal expression 'Be that as it may,' 27 times." The behavioral consultant was overjoyed that someone had learned so quickly that verbal behavior—what people say—can be counted as well. The consultant said, "We don't grade people in this workshop, but if we did, I would give you an *A+*."

Carl was having fun with the consultant, but he showed that he had learned the three essential skills for changing behavior: pinpoint specific behaviors that are observable and countable, count and record the frequency of those behaviors, and present the data to the frontline employee as feedback.

Measuring Critical-to-Quality Behaviors Is Essential for Improvement

Collecting data on behavior is the hallmark of the behavioral approach and essential for the highest levels of success. Why is collecting data about behavior so important? There are many reasons, but it is important to note that relying on subjective impressions about how often behavior is occurring is often very inaccurate. The Behavioral Quality Improvement approach is based on science, and uses the measurement of behavior to make decisions. Tracking a list of pinpointed critical-to-quality behaviors has many benefits for the organization, the customer, and for the individual performer.

1. **Behavioral data allow fact-based analysis.** After identifying critical-to-quality behaviors, the next question is, "How often are these behaviors currently occurring?" The typical answer to that question is not measurement based, because most organizations focus only on results, instead of the data about the behaviors that produce those results. Decisions are often a collection of guesses, beliefs, and assumptions. Actual behavioral data will put the Quality Action Team in touch with

the real facts. Behavioral data enable the Quality Action Team to know exactly how often the critical-to-quality behaviors are occurring and whether the behaviors are performed consistently. This will also allow a comparison among frontline employees, workgroups, shifts, and work sites.

2. **Behavioral data are actionable *leading indicators*.** Much of organizational problem solving is reactive. Poor results are encountered, and then the organization "looks in the rear-view mirror" to understand why the poor results occurred. This type of problem solving is looking backward in history to understand problems that have already occurred. In contrast, behavioral data are *leading indicators* because the data measures upstream behavior that could impact downstream results. Observing behavioral data lets the organization spot problems early and enables them to influence the behavior to prevent problems and improve results.

3. **Behavioral data permit effective feedback.** With behavioral data in hand, managers and supervisors can have more effective conversations with frontline employees about how they are performing. Often the simplest way of changing behavior is providing factual feedback to performers about their work behavior. Behavioral data give managers and supervisors the tools to have meaningful, motivating conversations about the work the frontline employee performed. In addition, managers can comment on any discretionary, positive behaviors the frontline employee performed that enhanced quality, and discuss behavioral changes that are needed to increase improvement.

4. **Behavioral data show trends.** Frontline employees will change their behavior gradually. So it is essential to "catch people improving" by spotting and acknowledging early improvement

in data trends. Numerical data about behavior let managers see and recognize subtle but real improvements and changes in the right direction.

5. **Behavioral data link people to quality.** Quality-improvement initiatives like Lean and Six Sigma fall short of expectations when they fail to systematically address behavior. The admirable quality slogan "Don't blame the person; fix the process!" can lead to overlooking the people side and neglecting the behaviors that help or hurt quality. Behavioral data enable frontline employees to see their contributions to quality. Behavioral data show frontline employees how changes in their behavior actually influence changes in quality.

Introduction of the Behavioral Approach to Obtain "Upstream" Safety Data

Those seeking to improve quality can benefit from learning how safety professionals measure behavior to reduce injury rates on the job. Traditionally, safety management relied on downstream result measures to track positive progress or indicate problems, such as recordable injuries. The behavioral approach was introduced in many organizations because analysis of injuries indicated that behavior contributed to injuries 70 percent to 80 percent of the time.

As safety managers reviewed injury data, they observed that frontline employees suffered certain types of injuries more frequently than others. When they looked at incident and injury investigation reports, they discovered that most often the injured frontline employees performed an unsafe behavior that led to the injury. In almost every incident, unsafe behavior was performed instead of a safe behavior. Safety professionals knew that increasing the frequency of safe behavior would dramatically reduce recordable and lost-time accidents. In Behavioral Quality Improvement, we are proposing the same idea for accelerating critical-to-quality behaviors during production.

Pioneering companies and behavioral psychologists developed a successful system for improving safety behavior. The key component of the system is to train frontline employees to observe their peers at work for brief periods of time using a checklist of "safe behaviors." The behaviors selected for the checklist are those practices that would prevent the most frequent injuries. These are usually simple behaviors, such as putting on safety glasses, attaching fall protection, or de-energizing a machine before performing maintenance.

Applying this behavioral formula to injury prevention has produced an average of 30 percent to 50 percent reduction in injuries in the first year. These data are based on international, evidence-based research across thousands of Behavior-Based Safety implementations. Also note that the behavioral approach to managing human performance has been used to improve work-site outcomes in every conceivable organizational function. The power of the behavioral approach is the foundation of Behavioral Quality Improvement.

Observing and Measuring Critical-to-Quality Behavior

To prepare for observing and measuring the critical-to-quality behaviors, the Quality Action Team will decide

- how often observations will be done;

- who will make the observations;

- the plan for tracking the process of observation and feedback.

Determining the frequency of observations. A good rule of thumb is that each performer should be observed and receive feedback (on the critical-to-quality behavior) *at least once per week,* either individually or as part of a workgroup. Observations and feedback may need to occur more often, depending on how often the critical-to-quality behavior is expected to be performed in the work process and if the behavior is new and unfamiliar to the performers.

Deciding who will make the observations. The Quality Action Team might propose that the observations be done by the Quality Action Team members, Behavior-Based Safety observers, supervisors, engineers, peers, and/or the performers. The Quality Action Team might recommend that the observers be volunteers or that observation be made part of the standard work of a particular group. The Quality Action Team's proposal will be based on the number of observers needed to complete the desired total number of observations, the expertise needed for observing, and the practical challenges of actually making the observations.

Creating a plan for tracking observations and feedback. On every shift, a designated person should collect the completed checklists and place them in an in-basket. The Quality Action Team member who has volunteered to collect the checklists then enters all the observational data into a spreadsheet or database. The spreadsheet or database will accumulate the observation data, day by day, checklist by checklist. The key is to have a cumulative record of the number of total observations in a workgroup, so that it can be analyzed, shown to the frontline employees, and used to make decisions.

The outcome of the observation-feedback planning should be a goal for the total number of observations per week, a list of observers and their individual observation goals per week, and a plan for collecting observation checklists and summarizing the data.

Supervisor and Peer Observations

If there is an existing Behavior-Based Safety process in place, the critical-to-quality behaviors can be inserted into the safety observation checklists. The Behavior-Based Safety observers can then check for critical-to-quality behaviors during their safety observations.

If the critical-to-quality behavior is expected to occur at predictable times that an observer can anticipate, then observer or supervisory observations are realistic. Observations require that frontline employees, working in sequence or in tandem, agree to allow the observation to occur. This subject can be introduced by the Quality Action Team or the supervisor in the area. If it is made clear that these data will not be used negatively, then chances are that you will get cooperation.

To record the data, the supervisor or peer has to physically check the behavior on the checklist. Checklists should be posted in plain sight; they function as prompts to the frontline employee that keeps him or her mindful of the critical-to-quality behavior. Since each organization is somewhat different regarding levels of trust between supervisor and frontline employee and between frontline employee and frontline employee, establishing supervisor and peer observation protocols is a site-by-site choice.

Self-Observation

Using self-observation, frontline employees complete the checklist themselves when they perform the behaviors, at their break, during lunch, or at the end of the day. Self-observation is particularly useful when completing the checklist aids the performer in doing the critical-to-quality behavior, when it is difficult for an observer to predict the timing of the critical-to-quality behavior, or when it is physically awkward for an observer to see the behavior.

Self-observation data has proven to be reliable. Our experience and available studies show that, most of the time, people will accurately record their behavior on a checklist. Sometimes managers are concerned that frontline employees just rush through a checklist without really giving a true report. In the positive process of Behavioral Quality Improvement, frontline employees are given plenty of time and encouragement to complete the checklists accurately. There is no threat of punishment if the self-recorded checklist data are less than perfect. The key to creating a reliable, behavioral, self-checking process is to provide the frontline employee with positive recognition for filling out the checklist. Do not criticize the quality, completeness, or unchecked behaviors. Frontline employees should feel comfortable that they are only documenting their work behavior, not "tattling on themselves." When managers get these reports, they respond positively to honesty, have open and honest discussions about causes of poor quality, and then develop plans to promote improvements.

Analyzing the Checklist Data

The Quality Action Team will want to analyze the observation data to answer three questions:

1. Are the observations actually occurring as planned?

2. What is the percent of observations in which the critical-to-quality behaviors were observed to be occurring as desired?

3. If the observations are occurring, and if critical-to-quality behaviors themselves are occurring, is there a related improvement in the quality results?

The Quality Action Team identified the critical-to-quality behaviors as the observable actions essential to quality results. The completed observation checklist is the evidence that the critical-to-quality behaviors have been performed. Therefore, the first analysis of the observation data is a count of the number of total observations per time period (such as per week) in each workgroup. The ratio of actual to planned observations each week should of course ideally be 100 percent. The Quality Action Team would benefit from knowing how many observations were made for purposes of feedback and recognition. The second analysis is in what percentage of the observations were the critical-to-quality behaviors actually observed to be occurring?

The final analysis is the comparison between the number of critical-to-quality behaviors performed and the quality results. If the Quality Action Team selected the right critical-to-quality behaviors, then an increase in those behaviors should drive a related improvement in quality results.

Posting the Data for Workgroups in Each Department

Each supervisor should be knowledgeable about the progress of his or her department. The supervisor should post the data about how many observations were completed on a bulletin board so frontline employees can see their self-observation progress. In addition, the supervisor is also responsible for mentioning improvement to individuals and workgroups that are making progress. All levels of management should make positive statements about progress at every opportunity. The next chapter will describe these Behavioral Quality Conversations.

What Did We Learn in this Chapter?

1. Once the Quality Action Team has identified critical-to-quality behaviors and created behavior checklists, the next task is to collect data about how often these critical-to-quality behaviors are actually occurring.

2. Behavioral data are essential to quality improvement. Behavioral data allow fact-based analysis, are actionable leading indicators, permit effective feedback, show trends, and link people's actions to quality results.

3. The Quality Action Team decides how often observations will be done, who will observe, and how the process of observation and feedback will be tracked.

4. A rule of thumb is that each performer should be observed and receive feedback on critical-to-quality behaviors at least once per week.

5. Observations may be done by the Quality Action Team members, Behavior-Based Safety observers, supervisors, engineers, peers, or the performers themselves.

6 BEHAVIORAL QUALITY CONVERSATIONS

Once teams are using the critical-to-quality behavior checklists, the Quality Action Team's next step is to encourage managers at all levels to effectively communicate with frontline employees about the behaviors. When managers use the opportunity to have a conversation about critical-to-quality behaviors with frontline employees, they also have an opportunity to discuss other topics about the frontline employee's work and performance. We call those extended discussions Behavioral Quality Conversations, and they are crucial to accelerating quality in an organization. Why is talking with frontline employees about the critical-to-quality behaviors so important? Because research shows that the conversations supervisors have with frontline employees make a big difference in frontline employee performance.

Judy Komaki, a renowned behavioral psychologist, conducted extensive research regarding the effect supervisory behavior had on frontline employee performance. She wanted to know what the most effective supervisors did to encourage high levels of performance. Komaki observed and categorized supervisors' conversations with frontline employees for thousands of hours, and then identified each supervisor's effectiveness according to performance results in their departments. Finally, she compared the conversations of the supervisors with the best-performing frontline employees against the conversations of the supervisors with the lowest-performing frontline employees.

Komaki found that supervisors and managers who frequently stop, look, listen and talk to frontline employees about their progress have better performing units than those who do not. The best managers stop and talk with frontline employees more often than low-performing managers. In addition, the best managers observe each frontline employee while working, and ask them questions about progress. Interacting with the frontline employee also provides more opportunities for the supervisor to make positive or corrective comments about the frontline employee's performance.

Komaki's research established a template for performance coaching. Traditionally, expectations for a supervisor's interactions with frontline employees were limited to the delivery of instructions. Komaki's research scientifically established a new paradigm for the supervisory role. Her research indicates that the most successful supervisors assume a "coaching" role with frontline employees. A coaching conversation requires spending more time talking with frontline employees about their daily work experience, and can be productive in many ways. One major result of these coaching conversations is that supervisors learn in advance whether there are issues related to the machinery, process, materials, resources, or any other factors that might influence product quality. In addition, these conversations (when done correctly) establish a comfortable atmosphere for the supervisor and frontline employee to have a balanced discussion of the work.

Behavioral Quality Conversations

The value of coaching conversations depends on the quality of the interaction. The tone of the conversation should reflect that the discussion is between two peers discussing the work. Frontline employees want their supervisors to be actively interested in their work, and when supervisors express their interest, it not only has a positive impact on the relationship, but on quality of work, too. When supervisors are not attentive to the frontline employee's work or actions, it leads the frontline employee to feel unimportant. In addition, if the work is not important enough to the supervisor to have a discussion about, it sends a message that the work does not have to be important to the frontline employee either.

Frontline employees judge whether you value them and their work by the active interest you show in the daily issues they encounter. You will not positively affect frontline employee job satisfaction and increase retention just by saying nice things to them; however, you will have a profound effect on those factors by becoming a performance partner—someone they can count on to help them deal with hurdles and barriers.

A Behavioral Quality Conversation can be any length appropriate for the supervisor and the frontline employee, often depending on how much the frontline employee has to say.

The purpose of a Behavioral Quality Conversation is quite clear:

1. Discuss critical-to-quality behaviors—prompting critical-to-quality behaviors not performed and providing positive feedback for critical-to-quality behaviors performed.

2. Ask the frontline employee about the technical aspects of the work; for example, equipment, material, and all elements of the process.

3. Discuss current quality results and any defects or issues.

4. Ask the frontline employee if there are any barriers to quality performance and if there is anything the frontline employee needs to improve quality.

A benefit of a Behavioral Quality Conversation is positive relationship-building. A human resource consulting company performed an analysis of job satisfaction and retention surveys conducted over the last 40 years. Their analysis corroborated that the single, most critical factor in frontline employee job retention is the supervisor-frontline employee relationship. A good relationship enables a supervisor to have positive influence on frontline employee performance. No matter what quality-improvement approach the company has set up, how much money was spent on consultants, and however much training supervisors have in Lean, Six Sigma, World Class Manufacturing, or any other approach, those managers still need to be able to form solid relationships with frontline employees and properly communicate to them about the critical-to-quality tasks, or all attempts at improvement will fall flat. Taking the time to have a Behavioral Quality Conversation creates the opportunity for the supervisor to learn from the frontline employee. The supervisor can discover things like

- what is going well and new ways of doing things that the frontline employee has adopted that could be shared with others;

- the opportunity to get faster, more accurate information about what is going on in the department that might affect the frontline employee and his or her work;

- problems the frontline employee may be having with equipment, availability of performance-critical information, availability of tools, materials, and maintenance assistance, and other job-critical factors;

- the presence of safety issues, such as conditions, equipment, or anything that the frontline employee perceives as a risk;

- whether processes or systems are helping or hindering the frontline employee's work;

- real-time problems the frontline employee foresees that may require the immediate involvement of other workgroups or departments.

Here is an example of what appears to be a good interaction between a supervisor and a frontline employee. Technical and performance topics are discussed, but it is missing some key coaching elements:

"Hi Pauline, how's it going today?"

"Fine," Pauline says.

"I wanted to remind you that when you change out the roller today, be sure you lock and tag it out, and watch the edge of the case cover. It's sharp and Jim almost cut himself last week. Do you need new earplugs?"

"I picked up some new ones just this morning," Pauline says.

"Did Ralph get those stage-two processors you needed to update your system?"

"I was expecting him to deliver 'em, but I haven't seen him," she replies.

"I'll check with him and make sure you get 'em before noon. By the way, when Cheryl comes by and asks you how you expedite services for our tier-one customers, would you mind telling her how you do it?"

"Sure, I don't mind," Pauline answers.

"Today at 2:00 PM we're having visitors from our largest customer tour the facility. You don't have to do anything. I just wanted to let you know they are coming through."

Pauline nods her head and replies, "Thanks for the heads-up."

The supervisor looks over at the equipment and says, "Yesterday, I happened to notice that you moved the rod component every time you reload. What would happen if you only moved it once?"

"I never thought about it; I'll give it a try," Pauline says.

"The idea you had about repositioning the tools worked for everyone except Alice and that's because she has an old machine."

Pauline smiles and says, "Glad to help."

"I'm going over to see if Dell needs anything. If you need me, page me. I'll ask Ralph to get those processors over here."

"The sooner, the better," Pauline says.

"See ya later."

This interaction contains several positives. One is that the tone of the interaction was collegial—like two peers conferring on work issues. The supervisor mentioned a safety tip that might help Pauline avoid an injury. He asked for her advice, which is something all frontline employees perceive as positive. He also suggested a change in the way she operated her machine that might make it easier for her, and gave her recognition for an idea that helped others.

This was a good exchange, but it was more like a transaction than an interaction. It is true that most managers would review this discussion between Pauline and her supervisor as positive. Compared to many supervisor-frontline employee discussions it was superior; however, a coaching interaction goes beyond the matter-of-fact information exchange. *Coaching requires asking questions and listening.* Here is an example of a better coaching conversation:

"Hi Pauline."

"Hi Jim."

"How is it going today?"

"Pretty good."

"Pretty good doesn't sound like real good. What kind of problems are you having?"

"It just seems to be one of those days. My machine is running slow and I have to keep a close eye on the settings. Without the two new processors I need, it just isn't running right. That means that some of the tolerances are sometimes off. I don't see them all because I have to look at the gauges so often. Then they go on down to Joyce and she lets 'em slide right through. Tony catches 'em at the final check and sends them back to me. It makes me look bad to Tony and the rework sheet makes me look like I'm not doing my job."

"That has to be pretty frustrating for ya."

"It's frustrating as hell. I'd like to line Ralph and Joyce up and kick them both where they sit down. They're putting my job at risk."

"You won't have to kick anyone. I'll take care of this and make sure it doesn't reflect on your job record. I know you've had to work extra hard to compensate for the machine problems. You may have a couple of pieces that went to rework, but you're still doing a great job."

Pauline smiles and says, "I appreciate that, Jim."

"Are there any other problems you're having?"

Pauline thinks for a few seconds and replies, "Well, there is one more thing. Maintenance is supposed to be calibrating the machine at the end of the previous shift. Every couple of days I get to the workstation and I see that they haven't been here. I tried punching-in early and calling 'em to come and do the job, but you can never get them on the phone."

"I'll get with maintenance on that. When you have these kinds of problems, page me. I'll come by as soon as I can. To reach our quality goal, we need to get these kinds of problems fixed faster. By the way, when I walked up I noticed you weren't wearing your earplugs. I don't want you going deaf on me."

Laughing, she says, "OK, Jim. I know it's for my own good. I'll make sure to use them every day."

"I see that you have been keeping track of the critical-to-quality behaviors on your checklist. This is really having an impact on our quality. The rejection rate is way down. Have you thought of any additional things you could do to improve quality?"

"No, but since I started focusing on these behaviors they have pretty much become a habit. I look at my checklist every day, but I really don't need to anymore. I have 'em in my head."

"Great Pauline! Page me if you need me. I'm going to have a talk with maintenance."

There was a broad difference in this interaction. Jim asked more *open-ended* questions. Open-ended questions, such as, "What kind of problems are you having?" enable the other person to provide more information. *Closed-ended* questions restrict information gathering. Questions like, "Did Ralph get those stage-two processors you needed to update your system?" as was asked in the first example of a sub-optimal dialog, doesn't lead to much information other than "yes" or "no." Any kind of closed-ended question, such as "Did you start-up on time today?" or "Do you have your Production Report form?" leads to a restricted yes-or-no answer. Meanwhile, the person answering the question has a wealth of valuable information that could potentially improve quality, but it remains untapped because the wrong questions are being asked.

The open-ended question, "What ideas do you have about ways to improve quality?" allows the frontline employee to discuss a wide range of potential improvement suggestions. If the supervisor had instead asked a closed-ended question like, "Do you think if we use Brand X instead of Brand Y we will get better material?" the answer would not have been as robust.

In the better dialog between Jim and Pauline, Jim managed to work in a few comments about the critical-to-quality checklist and get a read on how Pauline was coming along with it. Jim also did more listening than talking. In a Behavioral Quality Conversation, we want to use open-ended questions to collect ideas, problems, and opinions. The more information the supervisor has, the better he or she can influence quality production and services. Having asked the question, supervisors then need to listen, and reflect that they are interested in the answers. A good supervisor will maintain eye contact, hold a body posture that communicates interest, and even restate what is being heard. When listening, supervisors should not be looking at a cell phone or doing other things that might be distracting.

As you listen, do not rehearse responses or pursue an alternative line of thought. This is difficult because we tend to hear a few things someone says and that sparks a barrage of ideas that intrude while trying to pay attention to the speaker. Focus on the frontline employee and try to listen intently enough that you could paraphrase what the frontline employee said. When the frontline employee finishes speaking, repeat back your version of what he or she said to you so that you can come to agreement and an understanding of the issues at hand.

Delivering Recognition in a Behavioral Quality Conversation

Reflecting that you are listening to the frontline employee while speaking is always a good idea. Typically, people will say, "good," "uh-huh," "yes," or other words while listening to a person to communicate that the speaker's message is being received. These reflective and encouraging words acknowledge a frontline employee's performance, and strengthen your relationship within these Behavioral Quality Conversations.

A way to significantly improve your communication is to say behaviorally-specific statements like, "Great Bill! I think that adding that information to the work sheet will help the next shift get started without the confusion that we sometimes have." This kind of feedback works to let the frontline employee know that a specific behavior has added value. Keep in mind of course that if a frontline employee has already specified the behavior, such as, "I added several comments about recalibrating the gauges at the end of the shift to make sure that the evening shift can get kicked off smoothly," then one or two positive words like "Great!" or "That will work!" or "Good idea!" will be effective and positive.

Brief, positive phrases enable supervisors that are uncomfortable with longer statements to effectively recognize a frontline employee's extra effort. Positive comments like, "That will work," or "We should do it that way every time," or "That's going to save us a lot of time," are brief but they have a powerful positive effect on the supervisor-frontline employee relationship, and increase the probability that the frontline employee will continue to contribute extra effort to quality.

Coaching to Change Behavior

During a Behavioral Quality Conversation, supportive and corrective statements that influence frontline employee behavior can easily become part of the conversation without being negative. For instance, a supervisor can coach a frontline employee toward a new approach by saying, "You're expressing lots of good ideas about improving the machinery, Bill. Thank you! If you present maintenance with these suggestions, I'm sure they will implement the improvements. That is going to decrease the opportunity for quality issues and decrease the number of equipment problems you experience. Or a supervisor might say, "I'm not sure that's going to work for everyone Bill, but I like where you are headed with these types of ideas. I think you're on the right path even if they may not all be implemented." Coaching comments like these can be inserted into a Behavioral Quality

Conversation without changing the positive nature of the conversation.

What Did We Learn in this Chapter?

1. Critical-to-quality checklists can be used as a basis for Behavioral Quality Conversations.

2. Research has demonstrated that positive dialogs between supervisors and frontline employees lead to improved performance, fewer accidents, higher levels of employee engagement, and decreased turnover.

3. Behavioral Quality Conversations are characterized by supervisors asking questions, listening, providing performance improvement suggestions, discovering barriers to frontline employee performance, and strengthening the supervisor/employee relationship.

4. Behavioral Quality Conversations provide supervisors with an opportunity to mention—in a natural, genuine manner in the context of a general discussion—behaviors or results that the frontline employee has achieved.

5. Behavioral Quality Conversations also provide the supervisor with a context for mentioning behavior changes and improvement suggestions without being punitive or negative.

7 SENIOR MANAGEMENT'S ROLE IN BEHAVIORAL QUALITY IMPROVEMENT

Frontline employees are sensitive to senior managers' behavior. Senior managers establish the organization's values through what they say and what they do, and this goes beyond the decisions they make regarding promotions, raises, terminations, and bonuses. Every level in the management hierarchy watches the man or woman at the top. If the senior manager is focused on quality, you can be sure that every manager down to the supervisory level talks the talk and walks the walk.

When senior managers care about quality, they often try to manage it with established quality-improvement methods. It is important to keep in mind that most of the popular quality-improvement initiatives are expensive, both in terms of direct and indirect costs. Expensive management and frontline employee time is required to fuel the Lean Six Sigma machine. If senior managers do not see the return-on-investment from these types of initiatives, they are likely to abandon such expensive efforts no matter how popular they are. But because the senior manager's job usually demands attention to the bottom line, they are forced to find some other initiative that will help boost quality productivity. Often, senior managers look for the next "silver bullet" quality process that is being implemented by their competitors and the Fortune 500.

When senior managers no longer talk about an initiative or show any interest in it, the rest of the company begins to show less and less enthusiasm as well. Events are poorly attended and meetings are cancelled or never scheduled—basically the initiative dies a slow death through neglect. Behavioral Quality Improvement can help. The results from this approach have been documented for decades; it is inexpensive relative to the popular quality initiatives, and it takes much less frontline employee or management time compared to those initiatives.

Positive Inquiry

Throughout Chapter 6, we discussed how supervisors can use Behavioral Quality Conversations to improve performance. However, senior management's role in Behavioral Quality Conversations is not the same as that of supervisors.

Information is gathered in a constructive and encouraging manner but most often the conversation surrounds emphasizing and exploring successes, improvements, and asking questions that explore and expand the leader's understanding of the details of these events. They would as about those who contributed to the efforts and seek those employees out to have similar discussions with them.

Information gathered in this way has a positive impact on the frontline employee. Positive dialogs with senior managers help strengthen the quality culture and builds stronger relationship between frontline employees and all levels of management. It demonstrates that the manager listens to what the frontline employee has to say, and show interest in the frontline employee's information. At the end of this type conversation, the frontline employee feels good about the discussion and has a sense that the manager understood what he or she was saying.

Years ago in the book *In Search of Excellence*, Peters and Waterman proposed the now-familiar phrase, *management by walking around* (or *management by wandering around*). Some organizations refer to this as *floor walks, walk-abouts, field presence,* or *gemba walks*. Behavioral Quality Improvement suggests managers visit departments or workgroups where quality problems have been critical. Managers should also visit groups that are experiencing success with quality initiatives. At other times, managers may visit with Quality Action Team members or sample different areas at random to conduct a spot check on the health of the Behavioral Quality Improvement process. The idea in the Behavioral Quality Improvement method is to utilize walk-abouts as opportunities to assess productivity and reward critical-to-quality progress.

During positive inquiry the manager can discuss the critical-to-quality behaviors and the impact they have on product quality and customer satisfaction. The manager may address barriers and obstacles to quality performance that the Quality Action Team is tackling and the progress they are making. Positive inquiry is essential for Behavioral Quality Improvement because it enables managers to have conversations with operators and learn about their perceptions and experiences.

Managers Should Talk About Behavioral Quality Improvement

Managers should introduce the topic of quality at every opportunity. For instance, they can take a number of actions:

- Begin meetings with comments about Behavioral Quality Improvement and how it is progressing. Identify specific areas where positive results are occurring. Quote supervisors who have commented on the Behavioral Quality Improvement process.

- Ask direct reports about what they are doing to support Behavioral Quality Improvement. Are they talking with supervisors and frontline employees? Are they making field visits and walk-abouts and positively inquiring about frontline employee experiences?

- Ask all levels of frontline employees how the Behavioral Quality Improvement process is going. Do frontline employees like the process? Is the Quality Action Team actively championing the process in the field?

- Ask direct reports and frontline employees if barriers and obstacles to quality performance are being addressed and removed. Ask if there is anything managers need to do to improve or speed up that process.

- On walk-abouts, ask supervisors and frontline employees about the checklist data and quality-result data.

- During positive inquiry discussions, acknowledge—with a positive comment—any improvement accomplished by direct reports, supervisors, and frontline employees.

- Encourage holding a celebration for achieving quality results records. If a celebration is scheduled for a new quality-results record, be sure to attend.

- Communicate broadly across the organization quick wins on quality improvement.

How to Hold a Successful Celebration for Quality Improvement

Celebrations can play a powerful role in your Behavioral Quality Improvement process. Celebrations are events that provide recognition to a group that has reached a quality-improvement objective. If done effectively, it is an opportunity to excite people about their accomplishments. The Quality Action Team should develop a menu for a variety of celebrations that meet established company guidelines. It is good to pull ideas from managers and frontline employees within the department. The Quality Action Team should agree on the type of celebration, such as a pizza lunch, and the role each Quality Action Team member will play in the celebration

The celebration should be scheduled so that all the employees from the department have the opportunity to participate in and enjoy the event. It will require planning from the Quality Action Team. If possible, the celebration should take place out of the work area in a meeting room, lunchroom, or other area where the employees can gather and socialize with each other.

The purpose of the celebration is to recognize the quality accomplishment and to discuss how it was achieved. What helpful roles did frontline employees or managers play? How were the individual frontline employees able to help each other? What worked for individual frontline employees to help them succeed?

The understanding of these factors should carry over to other targeted quality objectives.

Try to get everyone involved in the celebration by creating discussion or Q&A. If employees are comfortable doing so, they may make brief comments to the group. The celebration should be for the entire department, shift, or team, including management and frontline employees who may not have had the opportunity to perform the critical-to-quality behavior being celebrated. If employees outside the department assisted, such as maintenance, consider inviting them. Employees should leave with a clear understanding of why the celebration took place and what behaviors frontline employees performed.

Managing Quality Improvement Checklists

One of the major problems with existing quality-improvement initiatives like Six Sigma and Lean is that they do not have a process for systematically providing positive feedback and recognition for participation, achievement, and sustainment. Without positive feedback and recognition, managers and frontline employees do not see quality as a priority. The activities and processes slowly drift and fade.

Surgeons, pilots, and astronauts use checklists to prompt them to perform behaviors critical to their success. During our work a few years back with one of the largest retail chains in the world, the President and CEO participated in a workshop in which we facilitated his development of a checklist of behaviors he believed were critical to his personal success. He wanted to precisely list the critical behaviors that led to the company's financial success. The checklist reflected the company's core values and positive management principles. He believed the checklist also reflected his personal commitment to continually improve his management skills. He performed these critical behaviors when he visited the company's retail stores and distribution centers around the world. He would often go on purposeful walk-abouts during which he talked with frontline employees at all levels.

When we revisited him several years later, he took us into his office to show us something in his top, desk drawer. He proudly pulled out his checklist, which was up-to-date and had been actively used. He opened a file on his computer and showed us several years of weekly checklists that had been scanned and placed in the file. Each checklist was dated and included notes scribbled on the back that prompted him to follow up on something an employee said or something he had promised one of the frontline employees. He said, "When we created this checklist, I knew that the items on the checklist were critical to my commitment to myself and to the company. I wanted to use the checklist to establish personal accountability for things I knew were important to do. In the last few years we have built several hundred new retail outlets and our sales and profitability have gone through the roof."

Quality Action Team-Manager Workshop to Create Checklists

To ensure that supervisors and frontline employees successfully implement Behavioral Quality Improvement and achieve improvements that will show up on the bottom line, each level of management—from senior managers down to frontline supervision—should have a checklist of the critical behaviors needed for management support. At this point, the Quality Action Team will have sufficient experience creating checklists of critical-to-quality behaviors for frontline employees and they can also help senior managers with this task.

The Quality Action Team will hold a workshop with each level of management in the organization or on the site. The purpose of the workshop is to work collaboratively with managers and supervisors to construct checklists of critical behaviors necessary to enable the success of Behavioral Quality Improvement and achieve the quality-improvement objectives. The workshop can range in length from a few hours to a full-day depending on the number of participants.

The Quality Action Team would review and discuss the bulleted behaviors in this chapter and adjust each level of management's checklist accordingly. To cascade accountability and ensure that each level of management receives feedback and recognition, each level would have a checklist item to review the checklists of their direct reports. Reviewing checklists and discussing Behavioral Quality Improvement is as important for senior managers as it is for frontline supervisors.

The Quality Action Team Tracks the Removal of Barriers

The Quality Action Team will be reviewing the observation data from supervisors, quality engineers, and selected frontline employee observers. All observers will be asking observed frontline employees how the Quality Action Team can enable them to perform higher quality work. In many instances, these will be easy fixes that can be facilitated by the supervisor, maintenance, or engineering.

In some cases, the changes needed to improve quality are going to require more complex fixes. Systems changes, process changes, equipment changes, and vendor issues are but a few of the types of issues that require one or more upper-level managers to get involved. The Quality Action Team will develop a tracking system that can be used to document frontline employee-recommended changes needed to improve quality and develop a procedure for passing the changes to the appropriate resources to review and act upon the changes.

Changes that require the signature of one or more senior managers should be delivered by a member of the Quality Action Team to the appropriate manager. The Quality Action Team will keep a running list of all quality-improvement action items and keep frontline employees informed about the status of action items initiated by their comments.

What Did We Learn in this Chapter?

1. Senior managers should support Behavioral Quality Improvement through positive inquiry. Positive inquiry suggests that information is gathered in a constructive and encouraging manner. The manager listens to what a frontline employee has to say, and has a meaningful dialog about the frontline employee's information.

2. Managers should visit groups that are experiencing success with quality initiatives. They may also visit with Quality Action Team members or visit different areas at random to conduct a spot check on the health of the Behavioral Quality Improvement process.

3. Managers should begin meetings with comments about Behavioral Quality Improvement, ask direct reports what they are doing to support Behavioral Quality Improvement, ask all levels how the Behavioral Quality Improvement process is going, ask if barriers and obstacles are being removed, ask about checklist data and quality results, acknowledge any improvement, encourage holding a celebration for achieving quality results, and communicate quick wins.

8 ADDING THE BEHAVIORAL APPROACH TO AN EXISTING QUALITY INITIATIVE

This chapter is about how to add a behavioral approach to your existing quality initiative to ensure successful and sustained implementation. The various brand-name, quality-improvement approaches—including Total Quality Management, continuous improvement, Six Sigma, Lean, World Class Manufacturing, and others—have provided excellent tools for analyzing the causes of quality problems and designing countermeasures to improve quality.

But imagine that you work in a process that has just been redesigned to improve quality. The list below may describe what you now experience. As you review the list, ask yourself how each new element would influence you. Would you be likely to engage in the new process or try to keep doing your job as you have in the past?

- Slack periods during your day have been removed.

- Opportunities for you to socialize have been removed.

- You must now operate several pieces of equipment—not just one—depending on need.

- You are now responsible for collecting and recording data.

- You must now communicate with people in other functions who have different backgrounds, training, and goals.

- You have additional responsibilities, such as cleaning and maintaining your equipment or inspecting your own work.

- You are now constantly on your feet when previously you could sit.

- You must now use a computer, tablet, or other electronic device.

- You are now expected to read technical procedures or diagrams.

- You must now write notes documenting your activities.

- You must now maintain your work area in a specific, orderly way.

- You are now expected to self-report your own mistakes.

- You must now point out the mistakes made by others.

- You are expected to admit when you don't know something and ask questions.

- You are given more work immediately upon finishing a task.

- You must now make judgment calls that previously were made by your boss.

- Your work speed and work tasks are constantly changed based on demand and workflow.

At least some of the elements of the new process might feel frustrating or annoying to you, or at least strange and different. You might be tempted to keep doing things the old way. Most often, frontline employees don't purposefully decide to revert back to old habits; it just happens as they try to avoid uncomfortable or difficult experiences like those listed above. These negative elements are often unintentional; the quality designers were not purposely trying to create a punitive process, but the frontline employees experience it as aversive nonetheless.

Frontline employees, supervisors, and managers can all encounter challenges in a new process: new ways of working may be difficult, errors may initially occur, and work may take more time. No matter how logical the new process looked on paper, if the human beings who work in the process encounter more negatives than positives, then their behavior will weaken or *drift* as described in Chapter 1.

Should You Add the Behavioral Approach?

Quality practitioners inevitably discover that while quality approaches offer useful analytical tools, *the success of a quality effort is not about the tools; it's about the people.* Should you add the behavioral approach to your quality effort? Think of some challenging projects in your quality effort. Have you experienced any of these situations?

- The operating team does not embrace a well-designed quality solution developed by your quality project team.

- Initial gains from a new process end up fading over time.

- Managers have limited success on quality even though they repeatedly urge frontline employees to focus on well-designed plans.

- Frontline employees seem to need repeated re-training.

- Quality proponents complain that the organization lacks a quality-oriented culture.

- Quality audits find the same problems again and again.

- Frontline employees do the minimum to pass the quality audits.

- More time and effort are spent on finding and fixing quality problems than on preventing them.

- A great deal of quality documentation exists—procedures, standard work, control plans—but the performance in the workplace does not match it.

- Projections about quality savings and return on investment do not seem to appear on the bottom line.

All of these situations indicate that Behavioral Quality Improvement is not in place but is definitely needed.

Include Behavior in Quality Tools

To add the behavioral approach to your quality effort, it helps to include behavior in the standard quality tools. In particular, add behavior to

- process maps;

- fishbone diagrams;

- quality action plans.

Show critical-to-quality behaviors on process maps. Often the first step in improving quality is to draw a current-state or "as-is" flowchart of the process. A team studying a quality problem draws a flowchart showing the current work process with an honest representation of problems with the process. The team then identifies ways to improve the process and draws a future state or "to-be" map that shows the new, improved set of process steps.

A process map is supposed to be a picture of the process, but if the picture does not highlight critical-to-quality behaviors, then those behaviors are unlikely to occur without a systematic process for ensuring they do occur.

To apply the behavioral approach to your quality effort, begin by making behavior visible on process maps. Identify the points on the process map where the critical-to-quality behaviors need to be performed. If necessary, add a table underneath the process map to list the critical-to-quality behaviors, the performers, and how behavioral data will be collected.

Once critical-to-quality behaviors are visible on a process map, the team can have productive discussion about those behaviors. How often are these behaviors occurring? How well are they being performed? What data are collected about these behaviors? What happens to frontline employees when they perform the behaviors? How can data-based feedback be provided to the performers? How can positive consequences be provided for improved behavior?

Look for the absence of feedback and positive consequences as causes of quality problems. To identify the causes of a quality problem, quality teams often use a fishbone diagram (also called an Ishikawa diagram) to illustrate the possible causes of the problem. The major categories of causes are drawn as large lines (large fishbones), and then specific causes are drawn as smaller lines (small fishbones). Most fishbone diagrams have a major category for People or Manpower. The team lists possible people-related causes of the problem on the People fishbone.

The difficulty with many fishbone diagrams is that they are incomplete regarding the identification of critical-to-quality behavior and the causes of off-quality behavior. Often the main cause listed on the People fishbone is "lack of training." It is true that lack of capability (due to lack of training or practice) is one cause of off-quality behavior. But if "lack of training" is the only People-related cause identified, then the proposed fix will always be training, re-training, and still more training (this can be observed in many quality projects). As stated earlier, training is not a total solution. Granted, training identifies what the frontline employee needs to do to ensure quality, but if the frontline employee does not perform the essential behaviors identified in the training, then the quality problem is not solved.

When constructing the People component of a fishbone diagram, always consider four more fishbones—in addition to training—that affect behavior:

- Critical-to-quality behaviors have not been defined and communicated.

- Frontline employees do not receive feedback about critical-to-quality behavior.

- The consequences that frontline employees experience after performing the critical-to-quality behavior are negative or neutral. There is no positive recognition for performing the critical-to-quality behaviors.

- The consequences for performing poor-quality behaviors are positive. It is faster or easier to do something else instead of the critical-to-quality behaviors.

If any or all of these four possible causes are observed, then the needed behavioral countermeasures are clear:

- Precisely pinpoint the critical-to-quality behaviors and communicate them.

- Provide data-based feedback frequently to the frontline employees about their performance.

- Provide positive verbal recognition to frontline employees when they perform the behavior.

Add feedback and recognition to quality action plans. Quality teams typically complete a quality action plan, sometimes called a DMAIC plan (Define, Measure, Analyze, Improve, and Control), to summarize their analysis, countermeasures, and implementation steps. The action plans list the changes designed to improve the process. The intention is that the process owner and operating team will behave as needed to control and sustain the new process.

All quality action plans should include plans for observations of critical-to-quality behaviors and feedback conversations with the performers. A change in process always means a change in behavior, and a change in behavior always requires feedback and positive recognition. An action plan to sustain or control a new process that does not include plans for feedback and recognition is a weak plan, because quality, after all, is about people!

What Did We Learn in this Chapter?

1. A quality plan may be rigorously developed, but if the frontline employees are not receiving feedback and recognition for performing the necessary critical-to-quality behaviors to implement the plan, then the employees will have difficulty changing their behavior.

2. Some ways to add the behavioral approach to quality tools are as follows:

a. Show critical-to-quality behaviors on process maps.

b. Look for the absence of feedback and positive consequences as causes of quality problems.

c. Add feedback and recognition to quality action plans.

9 MERGING BEHAVIORAL SAFETY AND BEHAVIORAL QUALITY

Behavior-Based Safety is a highly impactful approach for reducing incidents and injuries in the workplace. The implementation of Behavior-Based Safety has not only saved countless dollars for companies across the globe, it has also saved many people's lives. The Behavior-Based Safety approach has existed in one form or another for close to 40 years. About 25 years ago, informal standards relating to the practice of Behavior-Based Safety were developed as the result of prominent safety authorities writing articles and books about Behavior-Based Safety. The research on Behavior-Based Safety effectiveness has been published in leading journals by safety academics for decades, and the methods continue to be adopted worldwide.

Behavior-Based Safety consulting companies began the aggressive marketing of Behavior-Based Safety and speaking about the Behavior-Based Safety process at professional conferences and events. Soon literature from Behavior-Based Safety companies began showing up in every safety professional's inbox. Professional safety magazines and industry publications published regular articles and success stories about Behavior-Based Safety.

Fortune 100 companies started implementing Behavior-Based Safety, and employee empowerment became fashionable. Behavior-Based Safety was becoming known as an employee-driven, management-supported initiative with proven safety results while also having a positive impact on productivity and the bottom line. As Behavior-Based Safety results became widely publicized, the process spread through business and industry like wildfire. It was difficult to find a company of any size that wasn't in some phase of Behavior-Based Safety implementation.

Behavioral Quality Improvement shares many common elements with Behavior-Based Safety. Implementation of one of these approaches often paves the way for the other, allowing companies to get more value from their training investment. Often, the Behavior-Based Safety and Behavioral Quality Improvement initiatives can be integrated in ways that minimize duplication of effort. For example, critical-to-quality and safety behaviors might be included in a single checklist. Behavior-Based Safety and Behavioral Quality Improvement are very compatible, and when combined, create a return on investment that more than justifies the direct and indirect costs to sustain both initiatives.

The Core Elements of Behavior-Based Safety and Behavioral Quality Improvement

Most companies do not know that Behavior-Based Safety initiatives are resting on a scientific foundation that has been around for over 50 years—a foundation that has already been utilized by many companies to achieve amazing improvements in quality, productivity, timeliness, and customer service. The

Common Element	Behavior-Based Safety	Behavioral Quality Improvement
Pinpoint Critical Behaviors	Identify critical safe and unsafe behaviors	Identify critical-to-quality behaviors
Develop a Behavioral Checklist	Checklists customized to specific performers	Checklists customized to specific performers
Observe Frontline Employees Working	• Ensure observers can accurately identify safety-critical behaviors • Provide practice and coaching for observers	• Ensure observers can accurately identify critical-to-quality behaviors • Provide practice and coaching for observers
Provide Positive Feedback for Performing Behaviors	• Train observers how to have Safety Observation Conversations (SOCs) • Observers include positive comments about safe behavior in Safety Observation Conversations	• Train observers how to have Behavioral Quality Conversations (BQCs) • Include positive comments about critical-to-quality behavior in Behavioral Quality Conversations
Track Behavioral Data	• Track trends in safe behaviors observed • Compare trends in behaviors and trends in incidents	• Track trends in critical-to-quality behaviors observed • Compare trends in critical-to-quality behaviors and trends in quality outcomes

Figure 6. Common elements of Behavior-Based Quality and Behavioral Quality Improvement

foundation has five fundamental elements that can be applied to any organizational objective where human behavior is a factor.

The five fundamental elements of the behavioral approach are

1. pinpointing critical behaviors;

2. developing behavioral checklists;

3. observing frontline employees working;

4. providing positive feedback for performing the critical behaviors;

5. tracking the behavioral data.

Figure 6 shows the key components which form the critical dynamics of both Behavior-Based Safety and Behavioral Quality Improvement.

Most effective Behavior-Based Safety processes focus on specific safe and unsafe behaviors, create checklists of behaviors or practices that reduce the risk of injury, collect data through direct observations, and provide frontline employees with positive and corrective feedback and recognition for behaving safely. This means that if you have implemented Behavior-Based Safety in your organization or at your plant site, you have already started using the core elements of the behavioral approach as it is applied in Behavioral Quality Improvement.

Synergies Between a Behavior-Based Safety Steering Committee and a Quality Action Team

Most Behavior-Based Safety processes have a Steering Committee, which is a cross-sectional team of frontline employees, management, and professionals that processes Behavior-Based Safety data, facilitates the elimination of risk, and removes barriers to safety. The Quality Action Team that is created when Behavioral Quality Improvement is implemented (see Chapter 3) and the Behavior-Based Safety Steering

Committee are similar because they mobilize the removal of organizational obstacles to frontline employee performance, and interface directly with senior management to expedite decisions requiring capital expenditures and company-wide changes. They also interact with observers and frontline employees, collect and analyze data, and monitor the climate of frontline employee engagement and support of the initiative.

Even though their functions overlap, the Behavior-Based Safety Steering Committee and Quality Action Team should probably be separate groups. But if your organization has a mature Behavior-Based Safety process, you may choose to have one or more members of the Behavior-Based Safety Steering Committee also serve on the Quality Action Team. Experiences and skills that Behavior-Based Safety Steering Committee members can bring to the Quality Action Team include the following:

- How to pinpoint behaviors and create observation sheets

- How to train and coach observers

- How to set up observation frequency goals and schedules

- How to summarize and analyze observation checklist data

Including Behavior-Based Safety Steering Committee members on the Quality Action Team strengthens your investment in the Steering Committee by utilizing their Behavior-Based Safety skill set and applying the behavioral approach to a key organizational performance objective. It also revitalizes your Behavior-Based Safety process through the discussions they will have about how to merge the two processes to take advantage of overlapping functions.

Behavior-Based Safety Observers and Quality Observations

Behavior-Based Safety observers and Behavioral Quality Improvement observers are both performing the same basic function: directly observing frontline employees' job behavior to give them feedback about whether they are working safely or performing the critical-to-quality behaviors essential to the bottom line. Observational checklists can easily be adapted to both safety and quality. Unlike the checklists that are created to ensure that work conditions and equipment are in working order, safety and quality checklists focus frontline employees on critical actions that prevent either injuries or poor quality.

We should note that most BBS consultants recommend that the observation checklist items only address safety during the initial BBS implementation. This recommendation is made to help give special priority to safety and build acceptance by the workforce. That remains a general recommendation however and we have seen exceptions. Some companies have successfully included a few critical quality issues on the BBS checklist during the initial implementation. This approach is appropriate for organizations that have well established collaboration across level and in which employees are not resistant to the new process. In addition, we have seen other clients add quality into their BBS at some point after they have maximized the gains to be had in safety. Such companies are often looking for ways to expand the value of BBS. Quality is added as part of an effort to keep the BBS process ever green and keep employees engaged. Still other companies find more value in using a similar but parallel process with separate checklists and separate steering teams.

Existing Behavior-Based Safety Observers can easily be trained in the practice of Behavioral Quality Conversations (see Chapter

6). Behavior-Based Safety observers are trained differently depending on the Behavior-Based Safety model applied, but generally the training emphasizes presenting frontline employees with positive feedback and keeping the discussion of concerns positive.

Revitalizing and Reenergizing Your Behavior-Based Safety Process with Behavioral Quality Improvement

Every Behavior-Based Safety process is likely to need a "booster shot" at some point—something to help managers and frontline employees recommit and refocus on the process. Integrating the Behavioral Quality Improvement process into your Behavior-Based Safety process does just that: it engages everyone in applying their existing Behavior-Based Safety skills to a critical organizational objective. Observations and feedback become part of the total culture and not just part of the safety culture. More and more employees become skilled at both giving and receiving feedback. Quality problem solutions and quality improvements strengthen the organization's customer base, increase competitiveness, and improve the bottom line—all of which create a foundation for job security, raises, and promotions.

Integrating your Behavior-Based Safety process by applying its resources to quality is an obvious way to optimize the organization's investment in the implementation and sustainment of Behavior-Based Safety. The clear synergy and opportunities this brings to an organization are often not realized because many organizations' functional areas are maintained in silos of separation. In other words, safety and operations have different objectives and priorities and no forum exists for reviewing cross-functional opportunities.

Manager Support and Involvement

One common factor is shared by all successful attempts to change organizational performance—management involvement and support. If your managers are not actively involved and visibly supportive of your Behavior-Based Safety process, then chances are the safety process is struggling. In the Behavioral Quality Improvement process, the key objective of the Quality Action Team's manager workshop is to help managers create a checklist of behaviors which involves them in the Behavioral Quality Improvement process and ensures its success. Some behaviors that make it obvious to everyone that managers are interested in what is happening in the Behavioral Quality Improvement effort are the following:

- Using the Behavioral Quality Conversation format, ask questions about quality in their walk-about discussions with frontline employees.

- Review Behavioral Quality Improvement in any management meetings in which the topic of quality is discussed.

- Attend Quality Action Team meetings occasionally.

- Review quality-improvement results with direct reports.

- Ask questions about quality-improvement efforts and how they are going.

- Ask about the specific actions/operations that are targeted for improvement and how the Quality Action Team is planning to address those issues.

- Check to make sure that maintenance is expediting work orders related to action plans created by the Quality Action Team.

The Management Myth That Erodes the Bottom Line

A myth exists among senior managers and executives: they usually assume that quality problems can only be solved expensively. Large, fashionable quality initiatives that are very costly to implement and consume large chunks of manager and frontline employee time are the default solution for most large corporations. The assumption is, if it isn't expensive, it can't be a serious solution.

Training classes and workshops do not, in and of themselves, change frontline employee job-performance behaviors and/or solve performance problems, just as safety training alone is not an adequate solution to on-the-job injuries. Studies on "Transfer of Training" indicate that between 10 percent and 30 percent of classroom training leads to frontline employee behavior change on the job. Therein lays the myth perpetuated throughout corporate corridors, the myth that permeates large international corporations: "We will install Lean Six Sigma and that will solve our quality problems and lead to quality improvement." It is true that most Toyota Production System-derived quality initiatives install robust systems and processes. They often identify opportunities for frontline employees to improve quality; but they do not provide a systematic process for identifying, documenting, measuring, and encouraging new frontline employee behavior required to change past practices.

Ultimately, the only behavior-change process that has been demonstrated to work in hundreds of evidence-based, scientific studies is the behavioral approach:

- Specifically identify the behavior you want the manager or frontline employee to perform.

- Communicate the behaviors to the performers so that they know the behaviors that drive results.

- Place these behaviors on a checklist so that the performer is prompted by seeing it and mindful of the new behaviors.

- Use the checklist to create a measurement system that provides the performer and others with the knowledge the behavior was performed and the rate of improvement.

- Provide the performer with timely feedback and recognition for their efforts to keep the checklist and perform the new behaviors.

In training, you only discuss and identify new behavior that is necessary for organizational improvement. In the behavioral approach, you provide each performer and his or her manager with a measurement system to confirm they have actually changed behavior. Pairing the change with positive feedback and recognition creates the positive accountability that is needed to ensure that the trained behavior is adopted and performed.

In summary, an active Behavior-Based Safety process already in place will facilitate a Behavioral Quality Improvement implementation because the organization is already experienced in pinpointing behaviors, creating checklists, making observations, providing feedback, and collecting and analyzing behavioral data. Conversely, a Behavioral Quality Improvement implementation can re-energize a Behavior-Based Safety process by making the practices of performing observations and providing feedback become more thoroughly ingrained in the total culture.

What Did We Learn in this Chapter?

1. Behavioral Quality Improvement and Behavior-Based Safety share five fundamental behavioral elements:

    a. pinpointing critical behaviors

    b. developing behavioral checklists

    c. observing frontline employees working

    d. providing positive feedback for performing the critical behaviors

    e. tracking the behavioral data

2. Implementation of one of these approaches often paves the way for the other. The two approaches can often be integrated with minimal duplication of effort. For example, some companies may be able to add critical-to-quality and safety behaviors might be included in a single observation checklist.

3. Managers should create a checklist of behaviors that show the organization their support of Behavioral Quality Improvement, such as asking about quality during walk-about discussions with frontline employees and reviewing Behavioral Quality Improvement progress in management meetings.

CONCLUSION

The purpose of this book is to present a value-adding tool to quality-improvement efforts. The behavioral approach synchronizes with all of the major quality initiatives, enhancing their efficacy without interfering with or changing their core elements.

We are aware that many quality professionals may find it difficult to incorporate the human factor in quality management. Quality engineers and quality professionals are schooled to focus on "the process" as the key component in controlling quality and improving quality.

This book does not challenge quality principles; rather it exhorts quality professionals to take advantage of behavioral science to enhance quality initiatives by engaging employees to use the principles more effectively and providing them with positive consequences for doing so.

When behavioral science was first introduced to safety professionals, it met with mixed reaction. That was understandable; new tools are often met with doubt.

Now, Behavior-Based Safety is accepted by a large majority of the safety community and its value is seldom questioned. Implementing Behavior-Based Safety in organizations has significantly contributed to strengthening safety cultures through the distribution of safety management responsibility to all frontline employees. There is overwhelming research and data-based proof of Behavior-Based Safety's value in significantly reducing frontline employee injuries. Similarly, the authors collectively have 130 years of experience applying the behavioral approach to business and industry.

In many organizations, the behavioral approach has become a core component of management. Identifying the behaviors for success for all frontline employees and providing timely feedback and recognition for those behaviors are the centerpieces of management philosophy for many Fortune 100 companies. One of the largest companies in the world describes its management method as "reinforcement-based leadership."

So we humbly suggest that the quality community experiment with the process we have introduced. We have a great deal in common with quality professionals; we have spent many years of our lives dedicated to improving quality services and products for business and industry around the world.

We are not trainers—although training is part of our practice. We are first and foremost consultants. Like quality professionals, we are held accountable for our work and its results. So the advice in this book has been tested hundreds of times.

Conclusion

We understand what it means to introduce something new and put your credibility on the line. We believe we are providing you with a tool that will enhance and sustain quality initiatives and thus add value to your organization.

REFERENCES

Chakravorty, S. (2010, January 25). Where process-improvement projects go wrong. *The Wall Street Journal.*

Farris, J., Van Aken, E., Doolen, T., & Worley, J. (2008). Learning from less successful Kaizen events: a case study. *Engineering Management Journal, 20* (3), 10-20.

George, M. L., Maxey, J., Rowlands, D., & Price, M. (2004). *The Lean Six Sigma Pocket Toolbook.* New York: McGraw-Hill.

Komaki, J. L. (1998). *Leadership from an Operant Perspective.* New York: Routledge.

Michigan Occupational Safety & Health Administration (2011). Guidelines for developing a permit required confined space entry written program. Retrieved from http://www.michigan.gov/documents/dleg/deleg_wsh_cet5 330_346240_7.doc

Näslund, D. (2013). Lean and six sigma—critical success factors revisited. *International Journal of Quality and Service Sciences, 5* (1), 86-100.

Pay, R. (2008, March 1). Everybody's jumping on the lean bandwagon, but many are being taken for a ride—lean might not always produce the expected benefits and here's why. *Industry Week.*

Peters, T. J., & Waterman, Jr., R. H. (1982). *In Search of Excellence: Lessons from America's Best-Run Companies.* New York: Harper & Row.

Rosemary, R. F., & Wempe, W. F. (2009). Lean manufacturing, non-financial performance measures, and financial performance. *International Journal of Operations & Production Management, 29* (3), 214-40.

GLOSSARY

Behavior. An observable, countable action; anything someone does or says. Precise behaviors associated with job performance or job safety are identified. The objective is to increase the frequency of value-adding behaviors with positive feedback and recognition.

Behavior-Based Safety. An approach to safety improvement in which safe behaviors are identified, placed on an observation checklist, used by a trained observer to check a worker performing job tasks, and then used to provide the worker with feedback and recognition. The checklist results from all observations become a behavioral database which is used to measure improvement.

Behavioral approach. A scientific approach to strengthening behavior that includes five steps. First, identify the specific, observable behaviors that will improve a performance objective. Second, communicate the list of those behaviors to the relevant performers. Third, create a checklist to remind frontline employees of the pinpointed behaviors. Fourth, monitor frontline employee behavior with the checklist. Fifth, collect and present the observation data as feedback to the frontline employees and management. Provide positive recognition for improvement and goal achievement.

Behavioral drift. A phenomenon in which frontline employees or managers deviate from the prescribed "way they are supposed to do things," leaving out steps and adding their own twist to their jobs. For example, frontline employees may be expected to write detailed notes about production performance in a logbook during each shift, but in the absence of feedback and recognition for doing so, they might just jot a word or two.

Behavioral Quality Conversation. A conversation in which an observer or manager discusses critical-to-quality behaviors with a frontline employee, as well as other topics about the frontline employee's work and performance.

Behavioral Quality Improvement. The use of behavioral tools to focus on the "people side" of quality.

Checklist. An observation sheet listing critical-to-quality behaviors for a particular task.

Coaching. Talking to a performer about his or her behavior, providing measurement of progress, positive feedback and recognition for improvement, and corrective feedback for any needed change.

Critical-to-quality behavior. A high-impact, pinpointed behavior that drives a quality result. For example, "calibrating the equipment before starting work" may be an observable, countable behavior that has a direct, positive impact on quality results.

Feedback. Information to a performer about his or her performance, ideally about both behavior and results. Feedback can be behavioral, data-based, or both.

Leading indicator. An upstream metric that predicts downstream results. Behavioral data are leading indicators. For example, increasing the number of times that a team reviews work procedures before starting work may be a leading indicator of increasing the number of outputs passing inspection.

Measurement. The collection and tracking of data about behavior, results, or both.

Negative consequence. An event that follows a behavior that decreases the likelihood that the behavior will occur again. (The "negativeness" of a consequence is determined by the discouraging effect on future behavior, not by the intention of the consequence provider.)

Pinpointing. Precisely describing behavior in observable, countable terms. For example, "maintenance tasks performed as scheduled" is a pinpointed behavior that could be observed and counted.

Positive consequence. An event that follows a behavior that increases the likelihood that the behavior will occur again. (The "positiveness" of a consequence is determined by the encouraging effect on future behavior, not by the intention of the consequence provider.)

Positive inquiry. A way of gathering information in a constructive and encouraging manner. The manager listens to what the frontline employee has to say, and has a meaningful dialog about the frontline employee's information.

Quality Action Team. A team of members formed to identify and prioritize quality problems, pinpoint critical-to-quality behaviors that drive quality results, create observation checklists, develop plans to observe frontline employees, provide feedback on the behaviors, and monitor the results.

Recognition. Acknowledging individual or team improvement for increasing the frequency of a specific behavior or a performance result. Recognition can be as simple as a positive comment or as elaborate as an award banquet celebrating a quality-improvement achievement.

ABOUT THE AUTHORS

Jerry Pounds is President, International Division for Quality Safety Edge. Jerry has 40 years of consulting and coaching experience in applying the behavioral approach to quality, safety, and all areas of human performance improvement. He has designed and implemented hundreds of strategic performance-improvement initiatives in almost every major industry category including agriculture, aircraft, automotive, insurance, manufacturing, mining, pharmaceuticals, and retail. Jerry specializes in the development of behavior-based recognition systems and award-winning performance and quality-improvement initiatives.

Tom Werner is a Senior Consultant at Quality Safety Edge. Tom has over 30 years of- experience as an organizational consultant, coach, trainer, and facilitator. He has improved quality and changed organizational cultures through organizational behavior management, team effectiveness, process redesign, and continuous improvement. Tom has worked in a wide range of settings and industries, including manufacturing, refining, utilities, consumer products, banking, paper, and financial.

Bob Foxworthy is Vice President Latin America Market for Quality Safety Edge. Bob has implemented behavior-based quality in Mexico and the United States. An award-winning consultant, for over 40 years Bob has implemented behavioral solutions all over the world. Bob's specialties include organizational behavior management, Behavior-Based Safety, leadership development, executive coaching, improving customer-supplier alignment, and organizational culture change. Bob's industry experience includes oil and gas, hydro, nuclear energy, food production, paper production, marketing, sales, and general management, aviation, rail operations, heavy manufacturing, computers, textiles, waste management, government and police leadership, and small business development.

Daniel Moran, Ph.D., BCBA-D is Senior Vice President of Quality Safety Edge and has 20 years of experience applying behavioral principles in business environments around the world. He has conducted safety and quality-improvement initiatives in a variety of industries including construction, pulp and paper, manufacturing, and petroleum. Daniel pioneered the blending of Acceptance & Commitment Training with organizational behavior management in order to improve results in quality assurance, leadership consulting, Behavior-Based Safety, innovation training, and executive coaching.

Made in the USA
Middletown, DE
24 January 2023

23019469R00076